Cyclist4God

A Cyclist's Search for God

by Matthew Rodriguez

DORRANCE PUBLISHING CO
EST. 1920
PITTSBURGH, PENNSYLVANIA 15238

Dorrance Publishing Co
585 Alpha Drive
Suite 103
Pittsburgh, PA 15238
Visit our website at *www.dorrancebookstore.com*

ISBN: 979-8-88729-310-3
eISBN: 979-8-88729-810-8

Cyclist4God

A Cyclist's Search for God

Table of Contents

PREFACE

Fourteen years is a long time to wait although, to God, it is instantaneous. Knowing He was with me the whole time not only made it bearable, but also helped me learn about the blessing that was put on my life. I wouldn't have found out about that if I hadn't been in a near death accident.

From almost dying on the street, to almost dying in the hospital, it's evident God was with me. From a man working late to an obvious miracle in the hospital, the thought of God being with us is witnessed in this story. That wasn't the end of the gifts I would receive; He planned much more for me. If you have ever wrestled with the existence of God, then you should read this book; His existence did not end with the hospital or with the Paralympics.

I could have gone two separate ways: I could have just given up, or excelled. I chose the latter. I knew I would never be alone, and I would succeed with God with me.

> "The LORD your God is with you, the Mighty Warrior who saves. He will take great delight in you; in his love he will no longer rebuke you, but

will rejoice over you with singing."

Zephaniah 3:17

This has been an amazing journey, and it all started with a recumbent bike that I had no idea would be such a motivator. When I tried to excel my blessing with moving to the bike I'm on now without God, I learned that was a huge mistake. That taught me a lesson I would never forget. I wasn't in charge of the path I was on.

CHAPTER ONE
THE ACCIDENT

This is a trustworthy saying, and everyone should accept it:

> "Christ Jesus came into the world to save sinners"—and I am the worst of them all. But God had mercy on me so that Christ Jesus could use me as a prime example of his great patience with even the worst sinners.
>
> 1 Timothy1:15-16

No one, including myself, knew the night would end with a nearly dead person in the hospital. Sometimes you may not feel the love of God, but other times you do. It may have taken many years for me to realize that He did, but the important aspect of this was that I did.

I had been working three jobs at the time of the accident, that day just two. I had gotten off one job, spent time with my daughter, and then went to my second job. At my second job I was a waiter, but I am very good with people so doing it was really a blessing to me. Hours before the accident I was already tired, understandably so. So, I decided to relax with some friends after work; this was a regular occurrence for us to play some pool and have a few beers.

I had spent about two hours there because I went there about eleven P.M. and it was almost one. At around one thirty, last call had been called, so I knew we had another game of pool left. I did end up leaving around two A.M., probably around the same time the man who hit me left, except he was drunk. I was only twenty-nine years old and had no idea my life was about to change. I wonder, if I'd have known I would be in an accident, would I have changed anything from that night? If I knew what would happen in my future, there is no way, but then I would have.

After two A.M., I decided to go home. I was not drunk, but I probably should have called a cab. Like I just mentioned, if I would have known what would happen, I would have. I didn't want to spend all my money calling a cab, so I decided to drive home.

The bar wasn't very far from where I was struck by the driver, probably one to two miles. I was driving straight down the road and was hit by a drunk person speeding down Mollison perpendicular to the road I was on, Washington. He had claimed he was trying to evade someone following him, that was why he illegally ran a red light. He was driving in the turn lane, to my left, and hit me in the intersection. My truck was "T-boned" in the very front, though.

I was struck with such a great force that I was ejected out of the back window of my truck and landed on my rear but slammed the back of my head on the ground. It was a good thing I wasn't wearing a seatbelt because the truck "spun around" and hit a telephone pole. The driver's side was smashed, which could have been me if I would have remained in the truck. So really, I was saved from being smashed because I landed about twenty feet from the accident.

I wasn't lying in the road for exceptionally long when the ambulance came to help me. Emergency was summoned by the paramedics right after they'd helped me at the scene of the accident. At the intersection, where my car was struck, there was an automotive garage where a man was working late who called the emergency in. The ambulance came quickly and stabilized me; I had a long journey to the trauma hospital in Hillcrest, and I was in El Cajon, approximately twenty-five miles away.

What I've been told was I was so bludgeoned and bruised the picture on my license did not look like me. I was identified by a tattoo on my left arm by my roommate at the time. That was how my family and friends found out I had been in an accident and was in the hospital. So, it was a good thing my friend and roommate identified me.

When my family found out where I was, they came to be with me; my parents came immediately. My mom turned and looked at me, she could not recognize me and began to cry. My daughter was nine at the time and wouldn't find out about me until later that day. It was early in the morning, so I think my parents informed her mother around seven A.M.

I had many people come visit me: coworkers, friends, family, and even a couple I'd waited on the night of the accident. At the time, there was no way I could've known the number of people who'd come to see me, but it's humbling to know how many lives you've touched over the years. This happened every day for the four weeks I was in the hospital; my room was always filled with visitors, because everyone thought they were going to say goodbye to me. But never count out God; He loves to perform miracles.

When I had been in the hospital for two and half weeks, my mom called for a well-known pastor to come in and see me. Pastor Jerry Barnard came in to pray over me in hope it would help. I believe it did help me; besides you can never have too much prayer.

There were many people who came into the hospital room to say their 'goodbyes; my cousin Sherry was one of them. As she came in to say goodbye, she mentioned she was told to pray for me. Since we were in a hospital, she couldn't find a quiet place. So, she left the room and found a quiet place to pray. This was also one of the events that helped me. God is so awesome and powerful.

A couple days later, my dad called in a priest to give my Last Rights, now known as the Anointing of the Sick. It was after that when things started to happen. With all the prayers, and my cousin talking with God, you would think something amazing was about to happen, and it did. Everyone there was praying but I really don't feel they believed in the miracle God was about to perform. But that's what it was; no one can cheapen it. There is no way to explain this one.

While I was lying, completely motionless, in the room surrounded by family and friends, a miracle happened. I didn't have an out-of-body experience and was forced back into my body or anything like that, but something amazing happened. Now, there are a lot of people who would discount occurrences that involved God and say there was some other reason, but you can't with this. A huge rush of wind came into the room. I was told it felt like "the fluttering of thousands of angels' wings." They weren't hovering over me or perched above my bed, but it was a sign to many people God answered prayers.

Psalm 91:11 has special meaning to me now because of that moment. It states:

> "For he will command his angels concerning you to guard you in all your ways…"

This was a promise that did come true. We were in a hospital room. There was no way thousands of birds could have come in to mimic that force.

The next day, my dad made a request to meet with the head doctor. They were both state employees, so the doctor honored his request; he did not have to. Having him come to the hospital and intervene for me was a huge blessing and answer to prayer.

The head doctor conversed with the other doctors and asked what they had done to help me. One of the drugs I was given was propofol when I came to the hospital, which is used to slow the activity of your brain; less activity, less swelling. He was surprised at the amount I was still on which was normally lowered or not administered anymore, but mine did not appear to be. Whatever the dose was, it was too much. He ordered to get me off it right away. He had said, "That's enough to knock out a horse!"

I don't know your faith, but I know mine, and I know what happened was a miracle. There is no other explanation what happened that day.

After having a couple miracles happen for me, it was learned propofol had a half-life of about a week, so that was why I wasn't showing any progress or signs of life. Even though the doctor had ordered that I be taken off it, my parents were told I would either not wake up or wouldn't be the same. So, they were informed to say their goodbyes to me because I was going to be taken off life support.

But after my eyes were scanned by a device which checks for brain activity from the pupil created by the head doctor, they noticed I was not "brain dead." As the administered drug wore off, I began to get better. Every day I would show some different activity. Even after all the miracles that happened, there were some "nay-sayers;" more than likely, they were non-Christians, but I hope they aren't now. My family and close friends would not give up and still believed everything would be great for me, and it was, and is, a great life. God had another plan for my recovery; it would be a long journey, but a memorable one.

CHAPTER TWO
THE START OF A MINISTRY

My purpose for all this is not for me. I did want to be on Team USA for basically myself, but that changed. I really thought being on Team USA and going to the Paralympics would benefit only me, but I was so wrong. I will be honest, at first, I was thinking of myself, but God had another plan for me.

I would like everyone to know, regardless of your past, you can still be used. Do not ever underestimate God. He uses people who haven't lived a perfect life. He used Moses, who not only was a murderer, but had a temper problem. He used Saul/Paul, who was against the way and hunted down believers and killed them. I hadn't lived a perfect life either, but He used me.

As long as I can remember, cycling has always been an integral part of my life in my family. My uncle, my dad's brother, was a cyclist and got my dad involved. Before I was born, they went on many cycling excursions and involved other young people by running a youth group teaching the importance of cycling. My uncle even got his children into it; my cousin is a well-known, exceptionally good cyclist. So really, cycling was something that had been in my family and in my blood.

I grew up as any young kid would, except for the love of bikes. I'm not sure of the exact age, but I was on my first tricycle around the later months of two. I remember graduating to a big wheel around three. The pictures I have of me on a bike show the biggest smile on my face, but I'd imagine that would be true of anyone.

Not much is known after riding my big wheel, but I do have a memory of riding my first two-wheel bike. My parents were not wealthy, so I remember getting my older brother's bike as my first bike. The problem was it was too big for me, so I had to grow into it. It created a problem at first because my legs weren't long enough to touch the ground, but my dad solved that. He somehow fastened a seat on the bike with no seat post. To this day, I still don't know how he did that. The most important thing was I was able to ride my first two-wheeled bike. This is an especially important memory for me because it shows my determination to start riding a bike, even if it wasn't my very own.

I remember getting my first bike which, of course, was a Schwinn; it was a very popular bike at the time. I was probably around nine and very excited. Whatever it is, a car or a bike, having your own "set of wheels" can be liberating.

Something that was a huge part of my life was being able to ride to school. I was around nine at the time, and I'm sure my parents were nervous, but I rode with my older brother, who was four years older than me. It was around seven-to-eight-mile ride, and it wasn't that I couldn't do it, I was just young and my parents were nervous. At the time, it was nothing like it is now, with so much traffic and negative drivers, but since my brother was there protecting me, I feel that was the reason my parents were able to let me go.

I would do this every day for a few years until I started getting older. To me, there were more important things than riding my bike to school. I was so wrong. I started getting more involved in weightlifting, but only for physical appearance. Even at a young age, I was more interested in looking older and more muscular. The things that used to excite me, like riding my bike, were gone now. I still rode my bike, though, just more infrequently and for the wrong reasons. I was in shape, so I really liked to dress like a cyclist, in spandex shorts and a tight jersey. Now I do dress like that, but it's mainly because I'm a professional cyclist, and that's how other cyclists dress.

In high school, I started cycling again, but for the wrong reason. I was already in good shape, so I used to wear the tight cycling clothes to my advantage. I figured I would get more women looking at my physique than caring about my cycling ability. I was more worried about how I looked than really caring about how fast I was or the hills I could climb, nothing like the way I am now.

It was the same for many years, even after high school, I was more interested in women, but now that I was older it was younger women, over eighteen, though. I was around twenty-five dating nineteen- and twenty-year-old women, that was around the age of the women that were attracted to men in my shape. They were more interested in how men looked rather than their goals or aspirations, so I thrived with those women.

I was drinking, meeting women, spending money frivolously, having a good time and not caring about anyone but myself. I really did some immature things; I acted in ways I'm not proud of. I was, I cannot say particularly good, but I was a decent dad, but I was doing things a dad wouldn't typically do. I was nothing like the loving Father we have. After all the ways I acted, basically like I was number one, I was still loved enough to be where I am now. How I put myself before God, I'm incredibly surprised I'm not dead, and not just from the accident.

No matter what you have done or how you have treated others, God still loves you. I can attest to that fact. That is exactly how I acted when I was growing up; everything was all about me, but God still showed His love to me.

When I grew up, I was raised in the Church but not in having a relationship with God. I was Catholic but didn't have any structure. So, I was on the search for God. I went to a private Catholic school, but it was probably my fault for not having a relationship with Him. I still desperately needed a friendship with Him.

> "But from there you will search again for the Lord your God. And if you search for him with all your heart and soul, you will find him."
>
> Deuteronomy 4:29

I had no idea I was looking for Him, so I did not know how to find Him or that I was looking. All I know, that I didn't know then, is I was lost and needed a guide. I was not acting like a Christian, the way I try to do now. In my opinion, it was my religion. I felt whatever I did I would just be forgiven if I went to confession. The problem was I really did not understand confession; it was confessing your sins to God; I just didn't find it necessary to have an intermediary. So, it was probably me.

Growing up, I had no real choice because my family was Catholic, so that meant I was too. I do not regret it, though, because I wouldn't have the structure for the faith I have now. I spent kindergarten through eighth grade in a Catholic school which made me the person I am today. I was taught right from wrong; I don't know where I'd be now without that; probably dead or in jail! But it was during that when I started living for myself really, even though I did change churches.

One of my childhood friends invited me to go to his church, a Pentecostal church. I did not understand that either, but I was searching, and it was better than a Catholic church, I just wasn't being fed there. Going there was good for me. I learned more about God and the Church, the body of believers. I learned more about myself, too, but only realize that now.

Up to this day, except for being saved from my accident, I find going to a Christian Bible camp one of the greatest moments of my life. It was a Pentecostal Revival camp. The reason it meant so much to me was it was the first time I was searching for a relationship with God. At the time, I hadn't spoken in tongues, I actually still haven't, but I was praying to. Even though I didn't do it, it doesn't mean what I thought it meant at the time. There are "Spiritual Gifts," and some people have gifts others do not. It specifically says in the Bible not to try to obtain a Spiritual Gift; they are given to different people to help the body of believers. Now I know my main Spiritual Gift and use it to inspire the believers, to remind them to never give up. At the time, I had no idea what my Spiritual Gift was; it took until now.

Going to that revival camp started me on a path I didn't know I was on. I still behaved like a non-Christian, except for probably about two to three weeks. I ended up becoming a hypocrite like most Christians, doing the same others are doing and telling them it's wrong, that is the one thing I believe plagues the church. A lot of people act "High and Mighty" thinking just because they are Christians, they are better. In the Bible, it tells us not to think of ourselves as greater than others, but to be humble. That was one of the reasons I wasn't very fond of that religion—I should say that church—because not every Pentecostal church acts that way. That is something any church can be plagued with, but it was the main reason I didn't remain in that religion. I don't remember if it was long, but I did find a new church where I felt more comfortable.

I started going to Skyline Wesleyan, it was mainly for the youth group and the potential girls I would meet. That was where I went wrong, I was going for the wrong reasons. Which is one of the main reasons I wasn't there all the time in my high school years. I was not quite the person I am now.

I did grow in that church. I spent approximately twenty-five years there. I met some good friends and counsel. I belonged to a small group and went to a Sunday Bible Study, "Entrepreneurs for Christ." It was basically on having your own business or working for Christ, not human beings. But I still wasn't the person I am now, not until directly after my accident did I find my relationship with God. One would think after a life-threatening accident it would change everything, but it didn't happen until about seven years ago.

I think it was at Christmas 2013 when I learned about a bike that I could ride; it was a Catrike and had three wheels and was close to the ground. I looked for a dealer in my area, but couldn't find one, I ended up looking harder and found one. I talked to a man, Graham Butler, made an appointment to see him, and try out various bikes. I tried out a Terra Trike, a few different ones from Catrike, the villager, the expedition, the Pocket, and the 700. I also tried one from ICE, but I eventually decided on the Catrike 700 because it was designed for racing which was untrue because there was truly little racing with recumbent bikes. I was on that bike almost every day because it offered me freedom to go whenever I wanted. I used it as a catharsis and my time to be alone and talk with God.

This was when I wanted to tell people of what God did for me. I felt this was a great way to inform others of His love. I don't know, but it may have been placed in my head to start *cyclist4God*. I would expect it was from Him because it was available to use.

It took many years to get over the feeling of blaming Him for my accident, but I learned it was not God's fault. I searched and searched for answers to my questions—asking pastors why this happened to me, but I could never find an answer that would suffice. Working at a job for six years I did not like, where I constantly prayed to leave, was not very much help either. Now I realize working there was for my benefit, it was not a punishment. I had my own cycling class, and it also taught me to have more patience. Also, being able to discuss my dreams with people kept me trying to pursue them. But it is very sad for me to say waiting all that time lessoned my faith.

It really wasn't until I joined Team USA when my faith grew again, very sad to say. I would say my relationship grew to one hundred percent with God. I trusted Him more, but I realize now it's sad it took getting on the team for this to happen. I tell you this so you won't make the same mistake; this is exactly what God wanted me to do.

CHAPTER THREE
LOOKING BACK

I look back at everything I've been through—school, cycling, life—I know God has been with me the whole time. Every detail after my accident has been orchestrated to where I am now. Every part of my journey, whether it be big or small, was all known by God. He knew about all my successes and failures and that they would lead me to where I am right now.

This book is a reminder to you to never count God out. The plans He has for your life will come for sure, maybe not in the way you would expect. I never would've thought I'd be handicapped, but I still inspired people, probably more now than I would have. I never knew the plans God had for me; it took many years, but they came to pass.

> "For I know the plans I have for you," says the Lord. "They are plans for good and not for disaster, to give you a future and a hope."
>
> Jeremiah 29:11 NLT

There is no way I could have known what God had in store for me, or the end that was to come, and I don't know if it's over yet. Honestly, after my accident, I didn't know if it would ever come because I had fallen into a depression, understandably so. There is also no way of knowing if I will go to the Paralympics in Paris in 2024; it may not even be His will. My faith brought me to Japan in 2021, and either I will go again or God will open another door for me. Of course, I don't know if God has that planned for my life, I just take every day and every step as it comes; they are all blessings from Him, anyway.

If you ever feel God does not love you, remember my situation. I did not deserve all the blessings I received; I'm not talking about Jesus dying on the cross for us, because that's for everyone. I'm talking about my blessings of cycling and going to the Paralympics. The cycling was my gift I used only to bring God glory, going to the Paralympics is my blessing. Every day I wake up and thank Him for the life I have. Yes, I am handicapped but I have so much to be thankful for. There are many things I cannot do, but there are also things I excel at and have the attitude that I must try them. With everything I do or anything I want to do, God makes it possible. You need to come into agreement with Him and do it.

I came to an agreement with God about the blessings He has given me in my life. I began to trust Him more when everything started happening for me. Before it all started, I wondered if He had forgotten about me; my faith began to waiver. But as soon as I made it on Team USA, my faith became stronger, although it never should have decreased. Even before that, there were details in my life that now reveal His presence to me; it took all the blessings I'd received to realize this. You may not have the same blessings as me, but if you were to look back on your past, I think you would notice His presence. It can be something as small as failing at something a few times and then finally accomplishing it; it is His Spirit in you that gives you the desire to accomplish it by never giving up. That is the exact Spirit that has been in me over the years!

It did not happen right away, though; it took being tired of sitting around doing nothing that got me into this. I have never been the type of person to just sit around; I get very bored, that was placed in me. I would say I spent about a year and a half feeling sorry for myself, not really liking the situation I was in. That is what got me started. Right then and there, I made the decision to improve my situation, and God was in the driver's seat the whole time. God had placed the desire to never give up and it had been ingrained in me from a young age.

God had given me parents who did not like to give up. My dad, who grew up without a dad, learned from his mom never quit anything, that is why he's a graduate. My mom also grew up without a dad, but knew she had a Father in Heaven, and she excelled in her life as well. The fact is, with two great people God put in my life and the desire to never quit, I would never have given up!

The very first thing I did was get a recumbent exercise bike; I couldn't use a regular exercise bike because of the Ataxia I suffer from, lack of balance. It was a good time for me to start exercising again because I gained about thirty pounds. I had just been sitting in my chair watching television and eating, so the pounds added up. When I could finally exercise on my stationary exercise bike, you couldn't get me off it. Instead of watching television and eating, I was now watching and exercising. Rather than ingesting all those empty, dead calories, I was now burning calories. At first, it was only about three hundred calories at a time, if I was lucky, but after many months of exercising, it had grown to around eight hundred calories at a time. As you can imagine, I was not overweight for very long.

When I did master that, I had to move towards another goal. As mentioned, I need to move around or I get bored, I also do if I complete a goal. That was when I decided to start walking more and improve my gait and mobility. I was still using a wheelchair at the time and working with my therapist at using my walker. She had noticed my big improvement with using my walker and gave me the courage to start walking more without one. I had made the promise to God and myself that I would walk more. With that and mastering the walker, it was time to move to another goal of mine.

The biggest goal I had was to walk with nothing, but I knew that would be in the future. "You must learn to crawl before you walk;" that is a euphemism. I did not crawl. I did make another promise to God and myself, though, to use forearm crutches, but that would come after mastering using my walker which eventually came a few months later. I had been walking everywhere using my walker, including up and down my halls in the house. I would walk around a running track at a school by my house, stores—anywhere I could think of I was walking, but with a walker. The use of the walker opened many doors for me. It was good that I lived about three miles from the trolley station. I would walk there, go to the nearby mall, as well as the gym.

It did take a few months for me to master using my walker, but it did come. I was nervous to start using crutches because it would mean I would have to rely on my own balance and not my assistive device. What was the worst thing that could happen? I would fall, but what if I did?

"For though the righteous fall seven times, they rise again…"

Proverbs 24:16

I would just pick myself back up and try it again. I'm happy to say I never fell once.

My success with moving to one crutch was due to me walking down my hallway daily and my faith. Going to the gym to strengthen my legs and work on my balance helped me with my walking. All this had to do with my faith and all the hard work together. Knowing this, as well as going to the gym, would eventually help me to walk on my own.

But I was still using a crutch; it felt amazing, though. I spent over a month on that before transitioning to a cane. I still needed the support of a forearm crutch before I could move completely to a cane, although moving from a wheelchair to a forearm crutch was amazing to me. I really didn't care if I wasn't where I wanted to be, I was still progressing.

The biggest and final goal was yet to come. With approximately two years of hard work, and the faith that would get me to where I wanted to be, I started to walk with no assistance. I knew this day would come; I longed for it. With having the will to get out of the wheelchair and walk, knowing God was with me and would never leave me, I knew I would not fail. This opened so many different doors and gave me the ability to try anything.

With God and this, I know this is the reason why I am where I am.

CHAPTER FOUR
NEVER GIVING UP

It was 2016 and I had a chance to make a difference in the cycling world. I thought I would. I had the chance to go to Belgium and try to get the recumbent trike noticed for more competitions and possibly the Paralympics. I thought this would be my chance to glorify God more through what I was doing, but it was not His plan for my life.

I had to make all the arrangements for Belgium—a flight, transportation from the airport to the hotel, and my reservation for the hotel. It was a great thing I had a friend who could help me with the reservation to the hotel because I had no idea. Everything else— the airline flight and transportation—was all done by me. It was a good thing I had the money to do it because the whole trip ended up costing approximately $5000. Regardless of the cost, I knew I had to do this. I really thought this would open an opportunity for me and other riders to not only compete internationally, but to one day go to the Paralympics. I was excited to go and felt I was making a difference by making another classification for Team USA.

I informed the company I worked for of my plans and the eleven days I would need off. I can remember the excitement I had at the thought this would be my opportunity to leave this job and be on Team USA. I cannot explain the excitement. I had no problem getting the time off, and my boss had no qualms about me being excited about possibly leaving my job.

What seemed like forever actually came by quickly; I'm sure it was the exhilaration of being the one to make a difference. This would be my first time going to another country, and the very first-time recumbents would be allowed to compete in a race overseas. I was ecstatic this could be the start of a new life.

When the time came to leave, I had everything I would need to be successful in my journey. I had my bike all packed up in a makeshift shipping container, one hundred euros, and plenty of snacks for the plane ride and the time I would be in my room. It was good I'd brought snacks because not only was my flight long, but when I was in Belgium the time in between our meals was long.

When I did get there, I found my driver to shuttle me to the hotel which was about an hour and forty-five minutes away. I got there, checked in, and unloaded my bike so I could get ready to put it together. When I unpacked it, I noticed I had some brake issues, but thankfully the mechanic from Team USA helped me out.

After everything was done, I was ready to start training for the next day and to make history! I was the only one who was there on a recumbent bike at the time, so I had no one to ride with. I didn't let that stop me, I was there for a purpose and would let everyone know it.

I was there about four days before the race, so there was a lot of time to practice and learn the course. My only competitor came two days before the race, and we became instant friends.

But with only one competitor, my dreams of making a new category for para-cycling began to fade. I was not going to allow that to dissuade my feelings; I was there to show everyone, and the world, how important being on a recumbent bike was.

When the day of the race came, I was very excited to show how good I was as well as the importance of inclusion. But the horrible part was I only ended up having one competitor, so I needed to make sure I came in first place. Not to sound like a "snob," but I was a much better rider than the other guy. It wasn't a very long course at all, I think only about four miles. It was down the coast, on a flat surface, and back again. There were no difficult areas to look out for, no turns except to turnaround and come back. It was just a fast course, nothing difficult about it.

I did end up coming in first but, like I said, I only had one competitor. Because of the lack of interest by others on a recumbent bike, I wasn't successful with starting a new category. At the time I wasn't sure if this was God's best for me.

About six months after returning and being less enthusiastic about my chances of being on Team USA, I decided to try another route to get there. The same friend (Steve Peace) who helped me with the hotel reservation talked me into trying another way. Since I wanted to be on Team USA, I decided to try it.

My friend rented me a bike, an upright trike like I currently use, but it was me trying to go ahead of God. I thought if I couldn't get on Team USA or even to the Paralympics on a recumbent bike, I needed to try this way. At the time, that was the only way to make it there, and it still is.

I remember trying to perfect my riding ability using the upright trike. I tried every day to ride it, even going on a seventy-five-mile ride for Project Hero in Las Vegas with it. I'm happy to say I did not crash on that ride, but I did crash in Las Vegas the final time on that bike. It was then I decided to give up at the time, I thought for good. Even after multiple attempts and constantly crashing, I would not let myself give up. I had this feeling inside me to keep going; it was the determination put inside me. It was also knowing God had a plan for me, even though I could not see it. I went back to the recumbent bike thinking my chances and dreams would never happen. I was wrong, though.

CHAPTER FIVE
A NEW FRIEND

I met a friend, someone sent to me by God, on Facebook. It wasn't someone near my residence in San Diego; it was in Indiana. But since we were both devoted Christians, I would develop more spiritual growth from her. I believed she was sent by God for many reasons, but I thought it was for the wrong reason. I wasn't even trying to think of another way she may have been sent to my life except for love.

As I said before, God puts people in our lives for certain reasons; we never know why. At the time, I was riding my recumbent bike and racing as much as I could. I was training every day, except Sundays, and was incredibly determined to show more and more people how good God is. I had her complete support, both from her and from God; the way she encouraged me, I could tell God had sent her.

We spent about two months going back and forth with each other, not only conversing on Facebook, but also visiting each other in person. She also came to a few of my races at the time, once on the recumbent and once on my current bike. This was especially important to me because I wanted the support from the person I was with, hopefully a wife, but that was just a desire. But now it was evident to me that was not the reason she was placed in my life.

Around four to five months into our relationship, things changed for the better. I know now, but at the time I didn't. I had a friend who rented me a bike with an axel on the back, allowing two wheels on the back, a trike. It felt good to be upright again instead of so close to the ground. I felt comfortable riding on straight roads and hills but not on turns, that became evident. I had probably crashed about four times on it, and every single one was dealing with a turn. That was what made me give up on riding the upright trike at the time. It was not God's time for me.

I went back to the recumbent trike with her complete support, but I remembered her saying not to give up on it. I just shrugged it off. When I was back on the recumbent trike, it was exactly around the time of my last Redlands race on the recumbent. I invited her there because I wanted to have the support from the woman I loved. I had spent years watching other competitors kissing or hugging their wives after they had won; this was exactly what I wanted. More than likely, that was the reason our relationship moved so fast.

When I got home about two weeks after, I went to my favorite bike shop. I don't remember exactly why I was there; I think I was just in the area. My dad asked if I needed to stop, I did not but we stopped anyway, I just wanted to see the bikes again. I knew at the time I couldn't ride a two-wheeled bike; I was just drawn to them. Now I know God put that thought in my head. I was looking over the bikes, noticing the enormous prices on some of them, wondering if I could ride or even afford one. It was then that I found my first two-wheeled bike.

I didn't know it at the time, but this would start my new journey. My friend Greg, the manager at the bike store, mentioned he would give me a great deal on the bike. It was a carbon Fuji that was exceptionally light. I didn't know at the time how I would use it, or if I would. I had thought God did not have it in my plans to ever try riding an upright trike again and, of course, two wheels. But he was only going to charge me four hundred dollars. I couldn't pass that up. My dad said he would use it if I didn't. So, I ended up buying it, not knowing if I would ever use it.

I still was unsure about using it, but contacted my friend Steve right away to see if I could rent an axel from him to make my own trike, and he agreed. I was excited, but at the same time frightened to try this again. I had no idea God had a huge plan for my life. When I did ride it, I felt extremely comfortable, but was still uncomfortable with the turns. Still, I was riding it every day until I crashed on it for the first time. I ended up taking a day off and thinking about it.

I was wondering if I had made another mistake, if I was going ahead of God, if this wasn't His will? As you could imagine, or any believing Christian could, these thoughts raced through my mind. It was Jennifer (my ex-girlfriend) who grounded me, saying I shouldn't give up, so I didn't.

Around that time, I was invited to a talent camp for Team USA but wasn't sure I would go after my recent crash. It was also Jennifer who told me I needed to go or she would be mad at me. So, of course, I went. This was the start of my new journey with Team USA and what got me here. So, I will never regret meeting and falling in love with her. Never. I just wasn't paying attention to the real reason for meeting her. She was one of the people God had placed in my life to help me succeed.

That wasn't the end of our relationship; she was with me for longer than that. She encouraged me to keep going as far as I could. I went to Tennessee to participate in The Tennessee Paracycling Open (TPO), and she drove from Illinois to Tennessee to support me. But that was the last race she went to. Our relationship came to an end after that. It was about a seven to eight-month relationship, but what I ended up getting out of it was much greater.

CHAPTER SIX
A BIG CHANCE

It was now 2019, and it was going to be a big year for me, not to diminish the importance of 1999, the year of my accident. This year was going to be one of the years that would change my life; I had been praying a long time for this to happen. I had been feeling this year would be different than any other and it proved true. I was traveling to Europe for my chance to become a part of Team USA; it would be a dream come true. I had two opportunities to do well in my races, one in Corodonia, Italy, and the other in Ostend, Belgium. I had to podium, get first, second, or third, in at least two races; there were four total. So, to say I was nervous was an understatement, but I was happy for the opportunity.

I flew from San Diego to Rome, Italy first, which was a long flight—I think twelve to thirteen hours. When we arrived in Rome, we still had about a four-hour drive to our destination because it was in the countryside, not near a major city. It was an uninteresting drive, but I did get to see some of the most beautiful scenery I had ever seen at the time. To see the beautiful planet God gave us and how we have destroyed it amazed me.

When we arrived at a bed and breakfast my friend Steve had set up, it was in an area that was so beautiful, and the estate was gorgeous as well. I had a couple days to learn the first course; all the areas I had to be careful of. There were parts of the course that had uneven areas and some cobblestones, something I was not used to. I did that but I was taking in the scenery as well.

The day of the first race came, the "Time Trial;" it was a fifteen-kilometer course, and even though I was nervous, I was ready to do my best. I was going against some of the best in my category; unsettling, but I felt honored as well. One of my competitors, my friend Ryan, was the world champion at the time, and I would try my hardest to beat him no matter what. But I had a feeling I would not beat him, although I would have been happy to come in second place, but I ended up being wrong about the outcome.

We had to do two laps of the course, which was bad and good. There was a long hill towards the end, but I was known for doing very well on the hills, which ended up being to my advantage. Despite that fact, it was tiring and I did very well on it.

The way the time trial works: you do not race against other people; you are racing a clock. I don't care much for them because I like to be able to see if I'm ahead or behind my competition. This was not the case.

On my last lap before the hill was a flat area where I knew I could catch some speed. I did approximately twenty-six to twenty-seven miles per hour. That made me incredibly happy because it meant I could make up any lost time from my first journey around the course. Knowing God was with me the whole time helped with my energy, and that was much needed. If I did well in this race, it would help further my cycling career.

Right when I got to the top of the hill, I had to go to the right through an area in the town that was an alley; this was where the cobblestones were. It was another hill but not as bad, but after climbing the big hill it was taxing. This was the end of the race, and that made me happy. When I crossed the finish line, I was so happy it was over. I forgot to check my status and how many seconds I was ahead of the next competitor, which ended up being Ryan. When I did find out the results, I ended up beating him by eight seconds which meant first place. Words couldn't express how excited I was, and surprised, not only of myself but also everyone on Team USA.

The next day, I spent some time going over the course for the next race for the following day. It was almost the exact same course, except without the cobblestones. Instead of going to the top of the hill, you made a right turn about three hundred feet before the alleyway. So, the course was just as hard, except for the cobblestones. We also started in a different area, on top of a hill with an oddly shaped decline. I had to be incredibly careful of this because there were many sharp turns and I could have easily lost my balance and crashed, so I decided I would take it slow.

But when the next day came, I was not nervous or scared, I was extremely excited. Unlike the race from a couple days before, I would be racing against people not the clock, so I could see if I needed to speed up if I were behind. Saying I wasn't scared wouldn't be completely accurate I was scared about coming down that hill, twice. I just had to remember to be incredibly careful coming down it, and slow. I had a very smart idea after leaving the start line, that was to go to the right side and let everyone pass me. There was no need to take off very fast at first. I think there were only thirteen trikes, but they took over approximately three feet widthwise. Imagine thirteen tricycles together trying to get down a steep embankment, I wanted to be safe besides, I knew I would make up plenty of time on a straight-away.

When I made it down the hill, I came onto a road where I was able to go about twenty-seven to thirty miles per hour because it was downhill. I had to make a right turn after my decent, it was not a sharp turn but there was a rain culvert, so, to remain safe, I slowed down to about ten to fifteen miles per hour. After the turn, I graduated to an incline for around a mile and a half; the first time wasn't bad, but the second time was especially after doing the long hill.

What goes up must come down, right? After climbing that hill, the first hill, I started my decent. I came to a sharp left turn which gave me problems two days before, so I remembered to take it slow; I did not want to crash. The whole area was not what I was used to, not very bike friendly at all, not for a trike. So, re-alistically, not just that turn, but almost the whole race I had to be careful.

The next part I was really looking forward to, the completely flat area where I could go very fast and make up any time I needed. It was approximately three miles long of nothing but flat road, except for a couple round-a-bouts I had to slow down for, but after it was back to twenty-five plus mile per hour—and well, needed to because the next part was the three-mile hill that probably dropped me down to fifteen miles per hour, sometimes even slower.

Like I said, the next part was the hill, and it was in the back of my mind the whole time, dreading it. The first time was not as bad, but the second time was painful. Even when I was climbing it, the first time I thought to myself I have to do it one more time, and with less energy. I would be lying if I didn't admit to thinking, *Why am I doing this?* One answer, one word—love. It is great I train on hills non-stop, because it really does help me in times like these. But as soon as I got to the top and rode towards the finish line, I had one thought, *one more time!*

In the beginning and half my second lap, I was in first place. I wasn't getting cocky by any means, I was simply happy—tired, but happy. When I came down the hill and turned for the flat road, I was still in first, but I knew my competitor wasn't far behind. It was my friend and teammate Ryan, and I figured if I was going to let anyone get first place, I was glad it was him. On the flat road I tried to keep up with him, but I just couldn't do it. I wasn't giving up, not at all, I was just tired.

While climbing the hill the second time, I had him in my sights. If I were going to catch him, it would be now, because I was particularly good on the hills. The problem with that, so was he—not as good as me, but still good. I was not able to catch him, but I did do good enough to remain in second place, about forty-five seconds ahead of Spain.

The best part about the whole race was, not that I got to race in another country, but I was on the podium again, had made Team USA in one trip, and did not need to go to Belgium, but I went.

Corodonia, Italy, May 2019
This was from my second race when I came in second.

Picture by James Rodriguez

CHAPTER SEVEN
SOME RECONNAISSANCE

This was my second trip to Belgium, but it was very different from the first time, I was on a different bike. The first time I went I was trying to get recumbent trikes, a three wheeled bike closer to the ground, to be noticed and authorized for competition in the Paralympics, but it did not work. Besides, I wasn't very enthused to go because I had already made it on Team USA, so it wasn't necessary. But the trip was already paid for and I wanted to show the team I was an up-and-coming talent. Unfortunately, that wasn't how it happened; I think I was overzealous. I became one of the riders I normally stayed away from because they were too excited and became dangerous. I was not very excited to be there, at first, but when the day of the first race came closer, that feeling changed.

The excitement I had was building up greater and greater every day while I was out practicing the course with other riders. I could not believe I was considered good enough to be with professional bike racers from other countries; that was the same feeling I had in Italy. Even though, technically, I was not racing for Team USA, it felt good to be noticed as bike racer for USA. I was an independent bike racer, which meant I wasn't affiliated with a team, like Team USA.

When the day came for my first race, the time trial, a race against the clock by yourself, I wanted to do well, so I took off very fast. That was expected and not a problem for about a mile which was when I should've slowed down more. It was then that I came to my first real turn, a ninety-degree turn, and I didn't slow down enough. I wasn't experienced enough to control my bike or moving from my aero bars, bicycle handlebars that protrude in front allowing the rider to be in a more aerodynamic position, fast enough to use my brakes and went right into a barrier on the corner. Thankfully, I did not damage my bike, and a man helped me put the chain on the small chain ring. This was a problem because that was the slower of the two chain rings and my electronic shifter needed to be reset after a crash or wouldn't work, I was unaware of this at the time, so I probably lost about seven mph.

Knowing that I was going to be slower, I did not let that stop me, I tried as hard as I could and went as fast as the bike would allow me. I had traveled about three miles and was discouraged I couldn't perform to the level I was used to. However, I tried not to let it affect me.

While I was racing through town it didn't bother me much because that was the technical part I needed to go slower anyway; there were many turns. It wasn't until I was on the straight and flat road that I actually noticed the loss of speed.

As I was on that part of the course where I was supposed to speed up, rather than going twenty-five miles per hour I was doing about eighteen. I had to do two laps, and thankfully on the first lap I did not notice anyone passing me; that would change on the second lap. So, after I went through the first lap, I was going to make the first turn again, but I learned my lesson from the first time and lessened my speed. Although the town was mainly technical, there was one area that had a straight away, where I was passed the first time by Ryan Boyle who would become my teammate. What made that bad was since it was a time trial, we started thirty seconds between each racer, so I was behind that person by thirty seconds. After that, my standing went down from there.

It was when I got onto the straight and flat road when things got worse, but I had already expected that. I ended up being passed by four other riders, which was not that bad since I did lose approximately two and half minutes during my crash. But at the end of that flat road, which was an out and back, was the finish line and was ready for it after pushing myself more than I normally would.

When I did finish, I learned I came in seventh place because of the crash, but out of ten riders, that wasn't too bad; at least it wasn't last place.

The second race was in two days later which would give me a day to recover and gather some reconnaissance so I could improve my results. The course would be similar but a little different since it was not in town as much. However, it was mainly out in the open, so I would have to deal with the wind more; since Ostend was on the coast, the wind would be a major factor. In the town the buildings covered most of the wind—not so when we were out in the open.

I stayed with the "pack," group of riders, the whole race; I was trying to prove to myself and the other racers I deserved to be there. We had to do two laps like the first race, but the course was longer by double. But since we were allowed to draft each other—let the rider in front brake the wind for others—we saved a lot of our energy. As a courtesy to other riders, you would take the lead so not just one person would do it, everyone would. So, rather than just tire myself out I went with the group and stayed around nineteen miles per hour.

Although I stayed with the group to conserve my energy, I was beginning to get tired when I started the second lap. I honestly started to doubt my ability to stay with the group of riders, but that was not my personality, not even a little. I do not like giving up on anything, so I would tell myself that and pray for more energy. God never lets me down. What I prayed for and told myself came true because I stayed with them the whole time. I did not let the "pack" pass by. If I had, I never would have been able to catch up to them.

I had to stay with them if I was going to be able to either win or at least be on the podium. I was new to all this so I was not very sure when to take the lead and take off as fast as I could towards the finish line. Like I said, I was new to all this, I didn't notice them take off. Since they took off before me, I was two seconds off the winner, 2:05, 2:08, and so on from there. I would not get on the podium, first, second, or third, but honestly sixth place is not too bad, especially when you are just starting out.

Ostend, Belgium, May 15, 2019
This during my first race in Belgium a few miles after my crash
Picture by James Rodriguez

CHAPTER EIGHT
BAIE-COMEAU, CANADA

After my making Team USA, I was invited to go to Baie-Comeau, Canada. This was an amazing time for me, something I had wanted for many years. I had watched my friend Steve go to several places on different occasions, I was happy for him but jealous at the same time. Now, after many years of trying on a bike that would not get me there, switching different bikes, having a girlfriend at the time that basically threatened me (in a good way) and a friend who helped me achieve my goal, it was finally my turn.

From San Diego I went across the United States to Newark, New Jersey which, thankfully, I was only in the airport. I had around an hour and a half layover in the airport before I traveled to another country. It was not a very long flight to Toronto, around two and half hours, not even close to the four hours ride I had in the car. The only good part about that was the scenery; Canada was very beautiful.

When the four-hour drive was over, we came to the hotel and it wasn't very nice, at least the one I was in. We were at three separate locations, but since I didn't pay for anything, I really couldn't complain. It only took me a couple hours to put my bike together to be ready for my ride the next day. I needed to go over the course so I could be familiar with any hazards on the road. When I went over it, I didn't notice any hazards to look out for except the hill I had to go down with the ninety degrees turn. Even after going over it several times, I was still worried about it. I wasn't good at left turns, and coming down a hill before would make it even more difficult. I think I reviewed it four times, but did not want to do it too much and tire myself out, because coming down it meant I had to go back up it.

My first race would be a time trial of which I wasn't very fond of. Anytime I race, whether it's a time trial or a road race, I must be very careful because I'm traveling at a fast pace and must be very cautious around turns. If I crashed, I could either hurt my bike or myself. If I broke my arm, or suffer from a concussion, I would be out of the race season. So, being careful is extremely important to me.

We started about a mile from the hill, so I was able to speed up when I took off, not that I went very slow down the hill. I was probably going about twenty-two miles per hour in the beginning and about thirty to thirty-five miles per hour down the hill. But when I came to the turn, I slowed down considerably; it was probably around ten to twelve miles per hour. On my first time around, I did two, I learned I needed to slow down even more because I almost went onto the curb after the turn. So, I learned on my first trip on this course to be very careful on that turn.

The rest of the course had turns but with no hills; a lot of straight-aways I could speed-up around twenty-five miles per hour. But I did slow down before the turns. My bike is like a big tricycle, very unstable when I turned; I couldn't lean the bike over like a regular bike. The straight roads were where I was able to speed up and do as well as I did, but not like I wanted to. I ended up only getting third place this time, but it was a learning experience for competition. I had already started learning from the previous races in Italy and Belgium, this was just added experience.

I had to wait for one day to pass to race again. We practiced on the route some, but not much because it was on the same course, except for a few added miles. So, as well as spending some time on the course, maybe an hour, I also rode a bike connected to a trainer. We had to do the course twice again with the added course to make the full eighteen plus miles. This was also the race I liked a lot more over the time trial, the road race. I got to race against all the other bike racers. After doing a few races, I have learned to let the "hot dogs" take off first so I could do the race and not crash with them. With everyone vying for first place, it got very congested with all the trikes together.

Just like the previous race, we started a mile or two before the hill, but this time, after I came down the hill, I slowed down considerably. I also slowed down when other turns came up. There was a long stretch of land that was like a park; it was a long road, about a mile, where I was able to speed up. We were in a neighborhood community with some long and fast roads, but there were also a lot of turns, so I needed to be cautious.

During the race, I was close to one of the racers from Belgium, one person I learned after this race and many more, that he was not someone to be around. He moved erratically; he was dangerous to be around. Although this time was my fault for following him too closely. Most of the time it was no problem because I was close to him on straight roads, but corners were a different story.

We were in the town section where there were a lot turns, and yes, I was too close to this guy. I kept bumping his bumper bar (that's a bar that runs along the back of your wheels to prevent another ride from hitting your tires and causing you to crash). I learned it didn't prevent the rider behind you from crashing. When he slowed down at a turn, which I didn't do enough of, I bumped into him and crashed.

I ended up losing approximately three minutes to him because my chain came off and I did hit the ground. But just as I did before, I got back on my bike after putting my chain on again and went as fast as I could to try and catch back up with the group. I really don't know how fast I was going, but it was fast because I went a whole lap and caught back up with them. I can only thank God for the energy. But after going approximately eight to nine miles at twenty-seven to twenty-eight mph at full speed, I didn't have the energy to overtake them. It took all my energy just to catch up, but that was a huge accomplishment. I ended up coming in fourth place, but I did get the fastest time for the course. Even though I was the fastest—I believe twenty-two miles per hour for eighteen miles—I was a little upset I only averaged twenty-two. If I wouldn't have crashed in the first lap, it would have been about twenty-four.

BAIE-COMEAU, CANADA, August 22019
This is on my first race, the time trial
Picture by Casey Gibson

CHAPTER NINE
GOING INTERNATIONAL

I didn't get any time to rest before my next event. I came home for two days, just enough time to do laundry. I couldn't complain; this was exactly what I wanted. This was like the Paralympics, only for South America.

I traveled to Lima, Peru which was not that long of a flight; about three hours to get to Houston, and from there four hours to get to Peru. If you have ever been to Tijuana then you've seen Lima, Peru; it's very dirty and poor. The only good thing was a special lane on the freeways for the buses; it made me feel particularly important, like a president. The bus drive from the airport to the Athlete Village was not exceptionally long either, it took us longer to check into our rooms.

We ended up getting checked into our rooms about 4:30, almost time for dinner. I had five other roommates, all were track racers (they raced on a velodrome, an oval arena that is banked). I was the only road male road racer there. So, my friend, the World Champion Ryan, was not there, so I was expected to do well. I put my bike together after dinner ready to train and learn the course the following day. There were two different races: a time trial and a road race, but basically the same course. I wanted to do very well, so I learned about the course, the areas that would have the most wind (the whole course) and when would be a good time to break away from anyone. The course was right on the coast, and the wind would be a noticeably big factor.

One of my competitors was from Argentina, someone I had just beaten in Italy, so I was not too worried about him. I learned something about him this time; he was kind of a cheater! Regarding that: when a rider was leading in a pack with him and fell back, he never took the lead; he always wanted another rider to break the wind and expel all their energy, called "drafting." Then, at the last minute, he had all this energy to sprint faster than the rider. So, it wasn't that he cheats, he used strategy, but wasn't very courteous; he used other riders. But during this race, I didn't have to worry about him. There was no drafting allowed.

During the race, I passed Canada (for some reason they were there), Peru, Mexico, and thankfully Argentina. Since we were racing against the clock, and I'd started later than some riders, when I passed them, I didn't have to worry because I had already beaten them. I thought I did exceptionally well on the time trial, but there was one thing I did not like. The women were included in the result, but to make it fair, one hundred percent of their time on the course was against sixty-five percent of ours. As a result, instead of coming in first, I came in second place, but since first place went to my teammate, I wasn't upset.

The next day we had off and could go into town. I didn't know the area, so I didn't go anywhere. I didn't know anyone well enough on the team, and I was worried about getting a foodborne illness and, being in a foreign country, I did not have a hospital I trusted nearby. Getting lost in another country was a concern, and I didn't want to alarm the team administrator if I couldn't be found.

Two days later, we had to do some easy training on the course, because we had already done a race on it. It gave me a chance to go over the added length; I was unfamiliar with it. It would take about one and a half to two hours of traveling just to get there. It didn't seem worth it to spend all that time traveling just to do a two-hour training event for that. We could have just ridden a bike on a stationary trainer; we had some there.

The next day, we had to be on the bus by six A.M. to make it to the venue on time. Our race was not until one, so we had plenty of time to warm up. I ended up trying to take a nap because I was so tired. This time we had our own race, not mixed with the women. We arrived around 8:15 A.M. with the first race going off about nine. I don't know if I was nervous or cold, but I just couldn't fall asleep. Since I could not sleep, I just went over every detail of the race: bumps to look out for, the fastest line, my strategy, everything.

When the time finally came, I was ready to try my best, but I just wanted to get it over with. I kept my eye on the man from Argentina who stayed behind me the whole time, except for the time I got tired of waving him up to take the lead; he would never do it, so I just pulled over and let him pass. I ended up following but passed him again on the hill because I was a much better climber. We had to do that course twice, so I tried not to use all my energy at first. I couldn't help myself, though. There was a passion and desire to never be behind anyone. With cycling, that could have a negative effect.

On the last lap I was in the lead almost the whole time and, of course, he was drafting off me. When we had about three miles left, I pulled over again to let him pass because I knew he would never take the lead and let me draft. I let him have the lead until we came to the hill because I was really getting annoyed with him always drafting behind me. I realize now that was a mistake on my part because he ended up taking the lead and winning. He passed me up because he had all the energy. I was better on a bike than him, but he had more knowledge of what to do.

My time in Lima, Peru was slowly coming to an end, but not without a big celebration. The next day was a closing ceremony for the Pan-American games, for all the hard work, dedication, and devotion all of us had shown. It was extremely nice to be recognized. While being bussed through the town, it was hard not to feel advantaged when seeing all the poverty, and made me feel very guilty. All this money the country's government spent on us, but was not using to help their own citizens I thought was disgusting.

The next day was my flight back home. This had been the last event for the year. While it was nice to be able to race and travel from a very exciting and arduous year, it felt great to be able to rest. This would not be my final trip. I was going to a National Team Camp in February of 2020. Or so I thought. It ended up being a virtual cycling camp on Zwift.

Lima, Perù 2019 Me, Argentina and Canada
Picture by Rick Babington

Lima, Peru September 2019
This picture was taken in the Athlete Village in Lima
Picture by Rick Babington

CHAPTER TEN
HAVING PURPOSE

This is a story of my faith and how I believed God would help me. My faith did waiver at the beginning, but it came back stronger than ever. I don't want anyone to make the same mistake I made, so I pray you will learn from it. My purpose for all this is not for me. I wanted to be on Team USA for basically myself, but that changed. I really thought that being on Team USA and going to the Paralympics would benefit only me, but, thankfully, I was so wrong.

From the time I was growing up, everything I did was for my benefit. I wanted to inspire people, but it was always how it would positively affect me. When I started lifting weights, I would worry about what it would do for me. I wanted to increase my body mass to gain attention from women. When I was a teenager and became involved in cycling, it was only for what I could get out of it. It was never about this wonderful gift God blessed me with and using it for His glory. I wanted to gain the attention of the opposite sex; it was never about God.

But now I realize all this has come together to further God's kingdom. Being on Team USA has put me with a group of Christian brothers who have "lifted me up" and for me to do the same when needed. It also gives me the opportunity to share with people what God has done for me. This is what He wants, I believe. Going to the Paralympics just gives me further proof of how good He is to everyone. So, I never look on my accident as any loss for me, it is a gain. I didn't think someone like me could be used to help further God's kingdom.

This is where I made the mistake of underestimating God. I was not useless to Him. This is what gets me out on my bike to train, whether it's on the road or just in the garage. It isn't about what I can do for myself anymore, it's about how it inspires you and furthers your relationship with God. Not to say God intended this to happen to me to help inspire people. He would never hurt us. God's part in all this was to improve my situation, to show His power to people. I am just His vessel to do it.

I have a purpose in this life, and it is not for me. When I get to tell other people what God has done for me, I get this feeling God is smiling on me. I feel like I'm doing exactly what I'm supposed to be doing. I want people to know the truth about God, to know how loving He is. How He keeps his promises and gives you great gifts. A lot of people forget how much He truly loves us; I want to remind them. I think my situation is a perfect reminder.

I go forward in this because of faith, not worry. With God, I am always victorious. Whether it is my leg, my knee, or taking this vaccine, I know He is with me. I should never worry. Worry does so much harm to us. As Christians, we are told never to worry,

> "Therefore, I tell you, do not worry about your life, what you will eat or drink; or about your body, what you will wear. Is not life more than food, and the body more than clothes? Look at the birds of the air; they do not sow or reap or store away in

barns, and yet your heavenly Father feeds them. Are you not much more valuable than they? Can any one of you by worrying add a single hour to your life?"

Matthew 6:25-27

In this context, it does not make sense to worry. God already knows the outcome. You should never argue with God. Whether I win or lose, the outcome has already been determined, but that does not mean I do not need to practice. God gives me the ability to practice for an event and to do my best, and that's exactly what I need to do. I can worry all I want about this, but, like I said, it will only take away the enjoyment God has put into my life with this. My cycling is a gift from Him that He wants me to enjoy, that is one of the main reasons I keep on cycling, the other is because I can. God has given me an amazing gift. I love it, I know that it was from Him, so I need to bring Him glory and enjoy it.

It may be hard to believe but there are some days I really don't feel like riding my bike; some days I don't feel like even getting out of bed. Today was one of those days. Sometimes riding for Team USA can feel like a chore, something you're required to do and that's not the first time I've felt like that. So, in a way, I get tired of doing this for someone else. That is the way I feel sometimes, but what I always remind myself is why I'm doing it, and for whom.

This is exactly why I do not want to take the vaccine; I feel like I am being told to take it. If I want to keep riding, especially for Team USA, I must take it. I really should not be told to take it, only God can tell me, and He has not. I feel so good when I'm on my bike and get to talk to people; they get to see me firsthand. I know I would be much happier to do that for a living, rather than riding for Team USA. I want to have a cycling camp and help people achieve their goals; that is my goal, not for me to go to the Paralympics again. I feel if I go it would help provide credibility for me, but I will leave it in God's hands.

When I go out and ride my bike and talk with people, I feel as though I'm being led by the Spirit, I get invigorated. I feel as though God Himself is drawing me to certain people. All I can say is how amazing that feels. It's hard to explain unless you have a relationship with God. Therefore, I feel I should ride my bike outside not in the garage.

More than anything, I want to do what God has called me to do. With my handicap, and the seven plus years I spent racing and training, I feel I would encourage someone in the same predicament I was in to try as hard as I did and never give up. This is what I genuinely want. I don't want the gift of my cycling to be used for me.

The other night I didn't feel like going to my small group on Friday nights, but I have learned those are the times I need to go. I did not feel it earlier because I did not like driving all the way to get there, but at least I can drive. I made the excuse about the cost of gas going up, but that was just an excuse, a stupid one. I also made the excuse of my Achilles tendon hurting, and that it was cold outside. The enemy uses a lot of "lame" excuses to try and get you not to praise God or to be with other believers, but I did go and am very happy I went.

I'm glad I went because I was able to see the man I'd met about a month ago, the one extremely interested in cycling and sufferers from a TBI like I do. I have been thinking about the future of leaving the team and just doing this, it is the main reason I enjoy cycling, and took this as a possible sign. I just know doing this is what makes me incredibly happy, and I believe this is what I was called to do.

I still have the problem of furthering my career in cycling. Does God want me to so I can help others aspire to meet their dreams and give Him glory, or just stop? I'm starting to feel it's probably the first one because, like I said, this door is still open. I need to act in faith, believe this is God's plan for me. This feeling invigorates me. I feel the passion and desire burning inside of me again.

Meeting certain people I know God has placed in my life has been amazing to me, like meeting my second girlfriend. I was about to give up on trying to be on Team USA, but God sent her to remind me He was not done. Meeting my third girlfriend led me to where I am now, going to the Paralympics. Also, meeting a Christian author (Matt) gave me the feeling I should write this book; it has always been on my mind to do it; I feel this was confirmation. Right when you need the encouragement, God puts certain people in your life to remind you He's not forgotten about you.

When my hip started bothering me when I rode my bike, I thought it was over, especially after making it on Team USA. I was wrong again. I had some X-rays taken of my hip and my chiropractor noticed I had one leg longer than the other, the discrepancy was causing my pain. I had spent my whole life walking on two legs of different lengths. It not only affected my gait but also my balance. I ordered some lifts for the inside of my shoes to help with my walking. For my bike, it ended up being an easy fix, lengthening one crank while keeping the other one regular distance. So, there is always a reason for something, and God always has an easy fix.

The next thing was scary for me because this was something cyclists face because of repetitive motion with their knees. The different length of my legs could have had something to do with it as well. I started developing a swollen knee and some pain. I would take a couple days off which seemed to help, but when I rode again, it would come back. I was referred to a specialist after this kept happening.

There was a piece of covering over the bone that had been hanging on and causing irritation in the bursa sac and causing it to swell up. It turned out not to be an excessive problem, but it required surgery. But after the doctor removed my bursa sac and cleaned up my knee, everything seemed to be fine. This was the perfect time for this to happen since there was no racing for all of 2020, so I could recover. I have not had any problem with it since. God has an answer and a solution for everything.

During my recovery I met my recent ex-girlfriend. Again, I did not realize until now why God had put her in my life. We were both athletes and healing from recent surgeries. I wanted to inspire her not to ever give up. I also wanted a wife and had thought the situation was perfect, but that was not in God's plan. But having her in my life led me to accomplish my goal. So, I will never be sorry for meeting her.

Just as it was important for me to learn the importance of certain people in my life, it is also important for you as well. You may not be a professional cyclist, you may be a regular person, but God has a purpose for your life. It is up to you to find the people He has put in your life who will help you.

Now, it's easier for me to realize God has placed certain people in my life to get me to the destinations He's planned for me. But back in my earlier days it wasn't easy at all. I would say in the past eight years I have learned about not only finding the right people, but also praying for God to put the right people in my path who will help me get where God wants me to be.

CHAPTER ELEVEN
A WORLD CUP QUALIFYING ROUND

It took twelve hours to drive from Prescott, Arizona to Amarillo, Texas and it was very uninteresting; however, I was able to do some thinking. The only real time I get to do any thinking is when I'm on my exercise bike in the garage, and that's not very often since I mainly ride outside.

It's eight days away from when I race in Huntsville, but I leave in three days to drive there. I'm not nervous to race but I am for the outcome, what it means for my future. So, in that way, I'm nervous. I made a promise to myself if I did not do well, if I didn't make the team to Belgium, I'm more than likely going to retire. Well, not retire completely, just retire from Team USA. Yes, it did take many years to get here, and I'm happy I made it, but I'm taking this race as the answer I have praying for. I have decided I don't need to be in first place or go to the Paralympics, I'm not looking for any glory. I also don't want it to seem like I'm quitting, because that is not the case. I am going to try as hard as I possibly can, the result is up to God.

Well, today is the day I leave for what could be my last chance for Belgium and the Paralympics. I feel good about this. When I was riding my bike on the trainer yesterday, and the day before, I felt exceptionally good about it. In the past two days, I have averaged nineteen miles per hour, and the day before, nineteen and a half. So, I think I'm ready for this; if not, I'm happy with where I am. I just know that however I do, God is with me. I will do what He wants me to do. If I come in first, second, or third, it is what He wanted, not me. So, I don't feel nervous at all, I trust God. I also trust I took care of all the requirements I had to before the race, because if I didn't, I believe God is telling me something.

I'm disappointed with the traveling I must do. I must drive because my mom is afraid to fly. It's 1635 miles to get there, but we're breaking the drive up in three days. To me, it is worth it because I want my mom to go, plus my brother and dad; it's great to have the support of my family. This could be the last race I do in a long time, or even ever; I am not sure, so it is genuinely nice to have them there. They have supported me through the many years of racing on both bikes.

Our first stop will be in Santa Fe, New Mexico; it's 477 miles away and will take over six hours, but the big distance is tomorrow. We will be traveling from Santa Fe to Little Rock, Arkansas, an eight hundred-seventy-mile trip, almost twelve hours in the car. The shortest distance we have is Little Rock to Huntsville, Alabama; it is only three hundred forty-nine miles away, a little over five hours in the car. It's good I won't be driving long on that day because I don't want to come into Alabama tired.

This being the first race in about two years, and the last race here in the USA, I feel very confident. I get a chance to get back on the A team for Team USA, which means more money and more cycling opportunities. Not to mention, it will help with securing a spot for the Paralympics in Japan later this year. This will only be one of the races I will have to compete in to secure a spot.

I feel like I must have undeniable faith in God to do what I am doing. I'm here, getting ready to compete for a chance to go to Belgium and other places. I must have faith that this was given to me by God!

As the time to racing comes closer, I'm feeling more nervous, but this usually happens. Although, I was able to see how fast one of my competitors was today. There are not really any hills to compete with him against, but I noticed he was a little slower on inclines and turns. I'm not good on turns either, so I can't use those to pass him. I can use the inclines as an advantage, but like I said, there aren't really any.

Thursday was the last day of working hard, hard cycling. I must relax before my first day of my race, Saturday. It is a time trial and I'm not as worried about it as I was before because I got my bike up to over twenty-eight miles per hour and kept my speed up for a minute. I was able to do it more than once too, which is extremely good.

Sunday is a road race I'm a little nervous about; I'm only nervous because I'm racing the day before. I will be a little slower than usual because I'll be using a lot of strength and energy for my time trial, but I believe that is more important than the road race, so I want to make sure I do well in that one.

Today was my time trial, and I was ready for it. I had been practicing for it, but more importantly, I had been praying as well. I know that much of my success is because I pray and am always thankful to God.

I took off with a vengeance to come in first place. I studied all the street names I had to turn right or left on and remembered every obstacle I had to be careful with. On every turn there was a difference in the road, such as a rain gutter, or culvert, so that was something of which I had to be aware of.

Towards the middle of the course, there was a narrow road. It was one-way with parking on the other side. The good thing was it made the road a little wider, and thankfully it was the weekend and there were no cars; they would not be allowed to park there anyway.

I also made a promise to God to not let either Dennis or Ryan pass me. I started first, then Ryan, and then Dennis; we were in thirty second increments. So, if they would have passed me that would have added thirty seconds for Ryan and a minute for Dennis. I didn't want that to happen.

I think there were four racers who started before me, but I passed all of them in the first lap, except one, Michael, who had a real passion for cycling. Two of them were on recumbent bikes and could not compete with an upright trike, upright trikes are much faster than recumbents. All of them, even the people on upright trikes, stayed to the right so we could pass them.

I'm happy to say I did keep my promise; I wasn't passed by anyone. However, Dennis ended up beating me by twenty seconds, but I beat Ryan by a minute. I wouldn't come in first place, but second isn't bad.

Today is the road race, and we are allowed to draft. This could work for me or against me. The guy who beat me yesterday is new to the sport, so there is a good chance he doesn't know how to ride in a peloton—a train of cyclists riding close together. If I ride too close to him, I could hit his bumper bar, and ultimately causing myself to crash. That is the only concern I have for today, because I plan on coming in first. I'm pretty sure I already procured a spot going to Belgium, because the guy who came in first place did not register for Belgium; probably because he isn't internationally classified, not determined by a physical therapist for his type of handicap.

In fact, I made a promise to God I would try my best. I knew better than to say I would come in first. I was already tired and knew Dennis would try very hard. At least I knew I did not have to worry about Ryan as much. He wasn't performing as well; it was more than likely because he had a knee injury the year before.

This time I started with the other racers, but the riders are called up to the start line in the order they finished in the first race. So, Dennis chose first, then me, and Ryan; the other guys were last. I knew I did not have to worry about them because I beat all of them, and two were on a recumbent trikes, so they weren't in my classification.

I didn't have to worry as much as usual about Ryan; he normally went slow on the first lap, and on the second lap took off by himself. He tried this time but couldn't do it. We both worked together and tried to tire Dennis by not letting him move out of first place. That way he could break the wind for us, and Ryan and I could sprint at the end.

The whole race we tried keeping him in first place, but he learned what we were doing and would fall back to second or third after a turn. Although Dennis spent most of the time in front, our attempt failed. I noticed him tiring out, but I made the mistake of not taking advantage and gave him too much time to recover. There were two times I noticed that, but did not use that knowledge to my advantage, now I know. But we worked as hard as we could to keep him in first place as much as we could. It worked somewhat because when we came to the finish, he only beat me by about twenty-seven seconds.

Huntsville, Alabama, April 17
The race that would help further my career, in Huntsville. It was because I went to this race why I was selected to go to Belgium.
Picture by Loretta Rodriguez

CHAPTER TWELVE
OSTEND, BELGIUM

I made the team for going to Belgium, but I know I wasn't the best choice. That was fine by me because I was going and it would further my chances of going to the Paralympics. Even though I didn't want to go again, I ended up having a goal in mind this time.

If I did well in this competition, the chances of being selected for the Paralympic Team would greatly increase. So, even though I did not want to go, I did change my mind. Even though the thought of being sequestered in my room didn't sound appealing. But I figured this might be my only chance of ever going to the Paralympics, so I'd better change my way of thinking.

I started thinking God had given me this opportunity to go, with not winning in Alabama. When I had learned two of my major competitors would not be in Belgium, that really made me consider it even more. My chances of getting on the podium would increase substantially!

The higher I was on the podium—first, second, or third— would add more points to my standing and there would be no other choice than to choose me for Tokyo. Also, with ring fencing, they had to choose someone from my category to go to the Paralympics. So, the fact that I went to Belgium helped so much.

I came home after Alabama not knowing if I made the team going to Belgium, and I wouldn't know until I received an email. But when I got home, I acted in faith that I was already going, so I just kept riding my bike and assuming. I already had a belief I was going to the Paralympics, so I was training for that as well. So, I trained in the garage as well as against the wind; the garage to acclimate myself to the humidity in Tokyo, and the wind for Belgium.

After about a week I'd received the email that I made the team going to Belgium. I was so excited. I knew this year was going to be good! Learning, for sure, two of my opponents would not be there only further excited me. I had a feeling I would be chosen for Tokyo.

I gave reasons why I wanted to come which superseded why I didn't want to at first. We had to quarantine here for seven days before we could do anything; not that I would go anywhere anyway. Almost everything was closed, unless you went into a city; even then, everything was limited. I really didn't want to risk getting COVID anyway because that would mean I'd have to quarantine for two more weeks, meaning I'd have to pay for it myself.

Last night, April thirteenth, I got some bad news about my bike. The frame had some carbon damage, but I was told it would be okay to race on. The chain always came off and would get wedged in between the frame and the front chain ring, and I would try to force it out, not really knowing that too was damaging the frame. Now it must either be fixed, if possible, or I must buy a new frame. This could not have happened at a worse time, being overseas and not having any way to combat the problem.

Today is May second, and a verse came to me, even though the thought has been on my mind for days, even months.

> "On the contrary, who are you, O man, who answers back to God and dares to defy Him? Will the thing which is formed say to him who formed it, "Why have you made me like this?" Does the potter not have the right over the clay, to make from the same lump [of clay] one object for honorable use and another for common use?"
>
> Romans 9:20-21.

The whole morning this has been on my mind. I have prayed nonstop about this since last night. Ever since I shared a thought with some of my Christian friends I'm here in Belgium with.

It started with my devotional; I post it a day earlier to friends, so, it was tomorrow's post for today. It was about how God has His stance of acceptance toward you, His opinion. The author illustrates a story about an adopted child at the age of ten but did not feel like a family member. The child felt like part of the family when he was given chores to do.

That resonates with me. I have this feeling since I am on Team USA and have been invited to Belgium, I have been given my "chores." I also feel this has to do with the verses I detailed in the previous paragraph. I would be defying the Father if I didn't accept this invitation to Belgium, because this is exactly what I was created for.

This also has to do with my bike. It needs to fixed right now and may or may not fail during the race, which would mean I would not make the team for Portugal. But I'm not worried about it; it's in His hands. I would feel more like a son if I was invited. If I am meant to do well in this race, or my bike fails, I won't worry about it; every detail has been predetermined.

Everything is falling into place. If I do well here, I will either be going to Tokyo or Portugal, possibly both. The way this has "come into play" is amazing to me; it's a miracle, I believe. The way I was in second place in Alabama, but am here, and the other guy is not, amazes me. It's because he isn't internationally classified, which means he cannot race overseas, even better not in the Paralympics. This could be my time.

It's Thursday May sixth, the day I was looking forward to: my first race in Belgium. This was the third race of the year after taking off last year because of COVID. I did two in Alabama: a road race and a time trial, but this would be my first race overseas, so it was very important. The Europeans were generally faster and stronger riders than Americans, usually because of the wind and the hills. It was the time trial, a race I'm not very fond of. I must take on the wind by myself, so it takes a lot of strength.

Living in Prescott and it being windy, you would think going against the wind when I ride would help me tremendously, but that was not the case. I had been using the trainer in the garage more than I should have. I should have been training outside only for this one, but now I will just do as well as I can.

In my opinion, and this being my third race of the year, I was mentally ready for this but not physically. Since Germany and Australia are not here, I'm very fortunate; they are both stronger riders with wind than me, but I'm on hills. But even though they were not there, I still had to be careful of Spain and the Belgium racers.

Also, I took a year off because of COVID; I lost my speed and desire to compete. Now, after being invited to Belgium, my desire to race started coming back. Also, after receiving information I could go to the Paralympics and Portugal, I was invigorated. I thought about retiring last year because I didn't have any desire to compete anymore, but that started to fade.

When the time came for me to enter the start house, I went there without a fear in the world. I had now done this a few times before and learned there was nothing to be nervous about. All I must remember was to be safe around the turns. But there was one turn I was nervous about; the same turn I had crashed on two years before, but I knew how to take this time, so I would be fine.

When we started there were six racers who started before me, Belgium, and finally Spain. They started with the lesser ranked racers from the previous race. We took a year off, so I didn't know what race was used. I ended up passing every rider who took off before me, but I also was passed by Belgium and Spain. I was going quickly on the straight roads, but the problem was I was slower than them on the turns. They took turns wider than me, allowing them to keep more speed. I slowed down more because I would take them closer to the middle and farther coming out of them.

I could be upset with myself for coming in third, but I thought about it, and I'm not. I was happy about it for a couple reasons. I was alive and doing this! How many people could say they were doing exactly what they love to do, and bring glory to God? How could I be mad when I was going to a place like Belgium for free?

It was the day after the time trial and it was a resting day, although, I did go for a short easy thirty-minute ride. I just needed to get rid of any buildup of lactic acid in my muscles. I really worked my muscles hard yesterday, so they were sore. I needed to go out for a relaxing ride to flush my muscles out to do it again the next day.

May eighth, the second day that I had been anticipating. Maybe more than the time trial because I get to draft off other riders. I didn't burn all my energy because it was forty kilometers, and I may need to sprint towards the finish line.

My race started at nine o'clock in the morning, but I must start training at eight. I rode on a bike hooked up to a trainer to get blood and oxygen flowing to my muscles. I was extremely fortunate I got to race early because I must pack my bike up as well as my clothes and toiletries afterwards. So, the extra time I got to do this was greatly appreciated. I needed to take apart my bike and pack it safely so it didn't get damaged during transport; the baggage handlers weren't careful with it at all.

The race started on time, but there was an accident right away that I thankfully missed. I finished in third place during the time trial. My name was called after two, so I was able to get a preferred spot. I, thankfully, started with the other leaders in the race, that was why I avoided that crash with the other riders. It seems to me that riders who do well always avoid accidents.

As I stated, it was forty kilometers, two times around the designated course through the city, and down the coast. The wind was around thirteen mile per hour, maybe more. Through the city it wouldn't be so bad because the buildings usually covered it, but since the wind was going in the same direction I was heading, it actually helped me. For one mile the wind was behind me, but the majority was a headwind. But the last four miles were a crosswind because they were parallel to the ocean.

I had no problem staying with the group for the first lap, even around the turns. There were two other riders able to stay with us the first lap, but we ended up "dropping them" on the second lap. It felt great knowing I was a better rider than some other people from different countries, I had that feeling when I passed them.

Being able to stay with the "pack" was not a problem for me, but slowing down for the turns and increasing my speed quick enough to catch up with them really took a toll on me. On this course, there was a 180-degree turnaround. Every time we did that, I had to speed to catch up with the other riders. I believe the other riders from Belgium and Spain knew that and used that against me. If I planned on lowering my time, this was a technique I needed to work on. Because of this, I ended up coming in third place on the road race. That is not a terrible position; I still got on the podium, it also added points for my selection to go to the Paralympics. Of course, first would've been better, but God had a reason for me not coming in first.

Ostend, Belgium, May 2021
Going around one of the most technical arts of the whole course in
Belgium, even though this was the road race.
Picture by Martine Verfaillie

CHAPTER THIRTEEN
DIVIDED WE FALL

I was still going back and forth with the vaccine, but many of my teammates thought I should take it. I didn't like being told I had to take something I didn't want to. It was evident to me God had placed me here, so why would He do that if I might be potentially harmed? I also felt that going any further in my cycling career would be just for me. Did I really need to go to the Paralympics?

When I think about the door God opened for me, I feel that He wants me to show others how great He is. Being on Team USA did this, going to other countries provided the opportunity to tell people what God has done for me. In races, I not only get to show people I was good, but I also get to tell them how I got there. I cannot explain the feeling I got telling people what God has done for me. So, it wasn't fair that I would be required to take it or my teammates trying to get me to deny my feelings against the vaccine.

I hadn't been sleeping well at night. I believed it was caused by my constant worry about this. I had prayed about this. This went back further than praying about cycling, to the time when I was in school, when I really did not know what to do with my life. I didn't know what to major in while at college and it was really weighing on me, so I did the only thing I could do, I prayed. At the university, a new school for physical therapy might open at the time I thought was an answer to prayer, especially if it opened. It did, but I thought about it and didn't want to go. But now I'm thinking I should have.

There was only one real way to figure this out and that was to do it. I met another man, before meeting the book man, and he asked if I was in school. I explained that I felt like I had no time and no desire. With the time I needed for cycling, and the time I took for traveling to other countries, I wasn't sure if I had time. I knew if I were to go back to school, especially for physical therapy, I would not have time to finish this book or be able to train on my bike. This was a perplexing question for me, to determine whether I had gone far enough with my cycling and not go to the Paralympics or go back to school.

I wondered if I really needed to go, or if God really wanted me to go. If I went, I would have to take the vaccine, which I didn't want to or felt comfortable with. If I stopped now, I didn't have to take it; although if I went back to school, I would more than likely be required to take it. So, either way, I would need to take it, but what did God want me to do? I was going back and forth on deciding, but I had to remember a fact; God already had a plan for me.

In Jeremiah 29:11-13 it says: "For I know the plans I have for you," declares the Lord, "plans to prosper you and not to harm you, plans to give you hope and a future. Then you will call on me and come and pray to me, and I will listen to you. You will seek me and find me when you seek me with all your heart."

So, whether I took the vaccine and continued racing or went back to school, God already knew the outcome.

I'm sure I'd forget about this truth again, but the great news about that was I was already forgiven for what could be the wrong choice. That was unbelievable truth and great strength in times of distress.

That was exactly what happened the next day. I needed to remind myself, I am back to feeling very guilty about this again. After I read today's devotional, "Jesus, I don't want anything to come between us. Root it out, that I may be completely yours." (God's purpose for your life, March 16) I thought about my decision. I may have made my choice, and I thought I would take some time off, if not indefinitely. I had been asking for an answer to my prayer, but I wasn't completely sure this was it.

The past seven plus years I had wanted nothing more than to be where I am now. I had reached it; the goal was complete. Ever since I made the team, I had been wanting to go to the Paralympics, although it had been a lifelong goal for me to go to the Olympics. So now that I had a chance at going, I wasn't sure if it was me wanting to go, or if God wanted me to go.

I had to remember this: I didn't know the future; I didn't know what would be required of me. I needed to research this because I did not know for sure if I would be required to take the vaccine when I flew overseas, or just have to quarantine myself when I go. Maybe both?

I listened to a news program last night informing people what to expect when going to the airport. Everything was contactless. People were required to run their own license through a card reader. The TSA was not requiring a passport, which really made no sense. Everyone was supposed to have a test three days before they flew with the results, if not vaccinated. I had heard many conflicting arguments about the vaccine, but it was being pushed, and probably will be forced.

I did not understand the reason for taking it if I was healthy and did not have it. I stayed away from people and cleansed myself regularly. I washed my hands, used rubbing alcohol, wore a mask, cleaned my shoes, took vitamins; I was extremely cautious about that. I also knew that my body would fight it off, but it wasn't me I was worried about, it was other people. It was my family and people in my community; it would be extremely selfish to only worry about myself.

I couldn't allow any negativity to enter my mind. I was good, and the most important thing I had was God behind me. Whether it was going back to school or taking the vaccine, I must remember that neither were the goal at hand. Knowing God was with me was what kept me excelling and reaching because I knew He is faithful and wanted me to succeed. I was putting it in God's hands; I would use it as a determining factor whether to take the vaccine, also whether I should retire.

I wasn't giving up; it may have seemed like it, but I wasn't. I had reached a goal of mine, and that was to make Team USA. I think it was only a short-term goal. My long-term goal was to go to the Paralympics. I knew if God wanted me there, I would've gone. If it was His will for my life. So, I was practicing, I was being faithful to God, and I had a lot of faith He would be with me. The important thing was to know I was doing this for God and to enjoy it. That was all I could do: try my best and know that whether I win or lose, I was doing it for His glory.

CHAPTER FOURTEEN
LIFE AS A DESTINATION

Honestly, who would have ever thought I would be where I am? Not me, that's for sure. But that is how good our God is.

If you were to look at some of the times in my life, you would be surprised I am even alive or not someone who drank their life away. Just one word can answer that, mercy. I was shown so much mercy in my life, with being a young father, my bout with alcohol, my conceited lifestyle, my accident, all of it. I had done so many things I am deeply sorry for, but I had been forgiven for each one. Therefore, I ride my bike and tell people the good news; I cannot work for my salvation, but I want people to know how good God is.

There is one thing I know that is true, I would not even be doing what I'm doing without God in my life. I would have died in the accident. I wouldn't have had the hope I have now, knowing who my savior is and where my soul is going. So, I feel it is a job of mine to tell as many people as I can the great news of what we can expect as believers.

I'm asked all the time why I'm so happy and why I do this. This is what I say in my mind: "What would I possibly be doing right now if I wasn't doing this?"

Telling people about God's love for us all is the greatest fulfillment in this life. I honestly couldn't think of anything better. Being able to ride my bike was one thing, but I was improved to being able to race in different parts of the world. Really, without having God in my life, none of this would be possible. I have always had the feeling of being an inspiration for people, but know I am even more now. While the accident was not God's plan for me, what I am and doing now was.

I could be mad at the guy who did this to me, but I'm not. I forgave him many years ago. After many years of thinking about it, I am happy. I wouldn't be where I am now. Like I said, I don't place any blame on God for this. I have become a better person from my accident. I have learned to care for other people besides myself. That is why I explain to others what God has done for me.

It's all about gratitude, received grace, but not just that, I was very blessed. I look back at where I started, getting back to exercise on my stationary recumbent bike. Moving from that bike to a stationary upright bike was a huge accomplishment. Then using a recumbent bike on the road, now an upright bike. To top it off, being on Team USA and having a chance to go to the Paralympics. Regardless of how you may feel, you are blessed. Every day you wake up is a blessing. This something you must engrain in your mind.

Meeting people God has placed in my life has been amazing to me, like meeting my second girlfriend. I was about to give-up on trying to get where I am now, but God sent her to remind me He wasn't done. Meeting my third girlfriend also led me to where I am now. Meeting a Christian author (Matt) gave me the feeling I should write this book, so everyone needs to know God loves us all. It has always been on my mind to write about how God saved my life and blessed it. Right when you need some help God always sends someone's to intervene letting you know He has not forgotten about you. For me that was Matt, the Christian writer.

The first thing that started bothering me was my hip when I rode my bike. I thought it was over, especially after making it on Team USA. I was wrong again. I had some X-rays taken by my chiropractor and noticed I had one leg longer than the other; the discrepancy was causing my pain. I had spent my whole life walking on two different lengths; it not only affected my gait, but also my balance. I ordered some lifts for inside my shoes to help with my walking. For my bike, it ended up being an easy fix, lengthening one crank while keeping the other regular distance.

I went through a couple different different situations that worried me, I thought it was actually over. Just when you think that your blessings may be over with it usually means that God is going to do something amazing in your life, that's what ended up happening. No matter how long it takes or whatever you go through you need faith, mine ended up growing.

The next thing was terrifying because this was something cyclists face because of repetitive motion with their knees. The different lengths of my legs could have had something to do with it as well. I started developing a swollen knee and some pain. I would take a couple days off which seemed to help, but I would ride again, and it would come back. I was referred to a specialist after this kept happening.

There was a piece of covering over the bone that had been hanging on and causing irritation in my bursa sac and causing it to swell. It turned out to be an excessively complicated problem but it did require surgery. But the doctor removed my bursa sac and cleaned up my knee. This was the perfect time for this to happen. There was no racing for all of 2020, so I could recover from the surgery. I have not had a problem ever since then.

Then during my recovery, I met my recent ex-girlfriend and did not realize, until now, why God had put her in my life. We were both athletes and healing from a recent surgery. We both had the same dreams about our future, and our eventual mates, but that was not in God's plan, at least not for right now. At first, since we were both Christians not looking for love, the two of us thought we were putt together for it, but that was not the case.

Faith is believing in something that you can not see but you know is there but I already had evidence. I always have been a Christian, I just never lived, talked, or acted like one. I did not see the real purpose of going to church because I professed God, I knew He existed but that is not the only reason to go. It is also for fellowship, being around other Christians who believe the same; for friends who will lift you when you need to be and guide you back into the truth. I needed that; I just was not aware of it. If I wouldn't have had that network of friends, I might not be where I am, but I'm extremely glad I do.

This year and last one have been very trying for me; not knowing about the safety of the vaccines and whether I should take them, have really made me unhappy and lazy, and I also have not been eating like an athlete. I go out for my rides six days a week, but have not been very authoritative. I haven't been pushing enough or training myself hard; the Team Cycling Camp, made this evident to me.

I'm very tired today, a little too tired to go to my small group tonight. But when I went to my local gas station/convenience store to get my ice coffee, I saw an old friend. It is a long story, just seeing someone you did not expect to see can be God telling you something. I thought about this for a second and decided this was exactly why I should go to my small group. Be happy and give thanks in every situation.

I'm extremely glad I went tonight; I know God wanted me there. I met someone who suffers from a traumatic brain injury as well and is interested in cycling across America. I could be someone he can talk to. I also met a woman who takes care of her son who suffers from a TBI as well. I told her it took me twenty-one years to be where I am. I hope I encouraged her and him. You just never know where God wants you to be, you must listen. I am very glad I paid attention today.

It is good to have Godly goals in your life and to complete them, if you know they are from God it helps to fulfill it. When you finish that goal, it makes it much easier to complete the next one. From there, you never want to give up.

My very first goal was to ride a bike again, then compete, finally, to be on Team USA, all while giving glory to God. I have completed every one of those goals, but like I said, you must have new goals to complete. Just like Christianity, you never stop learning, but with goals you never stop giving up. A little advice: attribute it to God because you will never feel like giving up.

Because of Covid, I was unable to race all of 2020, but it turned out to be a blessing. I was able to not only get some much-needed rest, but I also met a friend. Not that God would hurt me, but I think this was a sign of needing rest, and as I said,

I met a friend who I believe was sent to me to help me through the recovery. My knee was becoming swollen, and I was worried my cycling was over. I was not in pain, but I knew I needed to see a doctor. During the height of the Covid pandemic, the doctors weren't seeing any patients, so I had a tele-visit over the phone. Prior to that, because I was waiting for a while, I had it drained by a physician's assistant. Thankfully, I was able to see a specialist, but even getting that took over a month, and my knee was growing. I was still riding my bike at the time, although just the trainer in the garage and at a slower pace; I could not just stop exercising.

I was incredibly happy, as well as my family, that I was going to see a specialist about my problem. I was diagnosed with perpetual bursitis, not uncommon for a cyclist because of the repetitive motion. My knee was drained from the accumulation of fluid. The doctor and I were hoping that would solve it, but it did not. There was some blood in the fluid, and he was curious what was causing it. But for the time being I was sent home for week and a half to see if that would help at all.

Not much longer after my knee was drained of fluid it started to accumulate again. I was riding my bike, but harder and outside, but that was not the cause of it. When I went back in to see the doctor, he tried draining it again with no luck. There was something inside my knee preventing the fluid to drain, which made the doctor curious, so he did a physical exam of my knee. He found that I had a piece of periosteum (a soft outer covering that protects and nourishes bone) causing the inflammation and excess fluid in my knee. He informed me the only solution was to have surgery to remove it and to remove my bursa sac. I wasn't worried at all, anything to get me back on the bike.

So, in about a month's time, I was scheduled to have the surgery. I was extremely excited because I knew this would solve my problem and I would be back to my training on my bike. The only hard part was not being able to ride my bike for five days which would not be an exceedingly long time for an average person, but I wasn't average, I was an athlete. I must be constantly moving, but that was where my friend Gloria came in.

I had met her prior to the surgery on Facebook; we were both athletes and going through recovery periods, although her situation was much more serious than mine. I was an extremely positive influence on her, but she was even more so to me. She had a fracture on her spine and needed surgery, so she needed prayer and asked me. That is how we met over Facebook.

So, when the time came for recovery, I had a friend to confide in and help me through the difficulty of not moving. I had someone who could understand my dilemma of not being able to exercise when I need to. These next five days were especially important for me to have her support, I could not do anything for myself. I had to stay off my feet as much as possible, except for using the restroom. I had to take a bath, something I despise, and hang my leg over the side to keep it dry. But Gloria understood what I was going through and absolutely helped me mentally, that is how I know she was from God.

When you are in any ordeal or time of trouble in your life you are never alone, God is right there with you and sends someone to help you. I was going through a hard time, but I was sent someone to help me. Regardless of whatever happens between us in the future, I will always cherish those five days. The fact that we were both Christian and single, I know that this time we had together was only for inspiration, it was God's plan to remind us of His divine plan. Not only I but her as well, took our meeting each other in a wrong sense, we both needed love at the time and were under the misconception that God had placed us together for that.

I am in the hopes of having her in my life for other things though. I do believe she was put in my life to inspire me and her, but I also have another idea why. I have a future goal of having a coaching and cycling camp and would need her business help.

I also have a decision to make that must deal with my future. I'm not sure what God is telling me. I want to make the right choice and think I have. Well, partially.

My first choice is whether I should stay in Prescott Valley, AZ or move to Flagstaff or nearby Williams. I love living here and don't want to move back to San Diego; it isn't a place I'd like to live. Firstly, it's dangerous in San Diego, as opposed to here to cycle and to drive. I have family there—my daughter and granddaughter live there and soon my grandson as well. My sister, cousins, aunts, and uncles. I won't let this make my decision; only God can make it.

The second decision is whether to start my cycling camp; that has to do with where as well. I know San Diego would be a more desirable place to have it, but it would also be more dangerous. I want to focus on handicap people, and they are usually close to the ground—at least I was when I started.

I was hit by a car in San Diego when I rode a low to the ground bike, a recumbent trike. So having a camp for handicapped individuals there would not be feasible, but I must listen for God's advice.

Another decision I needed to make is if should I retire after the Paralympics. I can't go any further; that is the highest destination for me. This could be the only time I can go as I would have to beat Dennis if he gets confirmed with his classification, as well as my friend Ryan Boyle; I know he'll try to make the next one. I'm going to wait on God and not worry about it, because if He wants me to retire, I will.

What am I going to do with myself in the future? I know better than to think about the future; it's not in my hands. God has taken care of me my whole life and has especially blessed me the past three years. I have never had to worry about what to eat, what to wear, where to live, anything; God has taken care of me. But right now, I cannot think about that. It's not like I'm hoping and praying for what I have now. I've already done that in the past. Even though I know not to think or even worry about the future, I'm not perfect. I still do.

I'm trying extremely hard not to let any of the future bother me. I have no control over it, somewhat. What I mean is I have no control of my success or failure. I could move back to San Diego and return to school for physical therapy, but there is no promise of success even if it might be God's will for my life. It's something I would need to work on, just like living here and start-ing a cycling camp.

Even though I think God may want me to do either one, that still doesn't determine my success. It does though if I work at my goal to please God. With all that has happened to me in the past few months, I'm starting to believe that running a cycling camp might be what God wants me to do. If God wants me to do this, I would be successful at it, but in the way that I would be working for God, not becoming rich at it.

I have three weeks and one day until I leave for Japan. I still find it surreal I'm going or that I'm even here. I even ordered a shirt with my name on it. When will I ever be able to buy a shirt with my name on it? I have an opportunity to make some money with Team USA by selling some T-shirts with my name on them: seven dollars per shirt. I have more opportunities to make some more money, other than with T-shirts.

I know I'm good, but I don't feel worthy enough to be with some of the athletes here. I feel blessed, but to be here with what I consider "real athletes" is unbelievable. If you have ever felt unworthy of being somewhere, that's how I feel right now.

I'm leaving early today to start my long journey home to Arizona from Beaumont, Solvang. Today marks three weeks until I leave for Japan. I'm excited to go. Now I must return home and get ready for this. I don't know how I will do this. I don't want to ride too hard, I know I can recover in time, but I don't want to use any energy. For today, I'm just going to sit and relax and try not to bored.

One thing I'm pretty sure I'll do is mainly ride in the garage. I have a couple reasons for this. A friend of mine was struck by a car and lost her invitation to go to Japan because the doctor did not clear her. I don't want that to happen to me. I also want to train in the heat so I can acclimate myself to the heat and humidity there. My plan will be to train in the garage with the door closed.

It is August third, and the time just keeps getting closer and closer. Even though I'm getting emails from the director in Paracycling, I still haven't accepted the fact I'm going to the Paralympics. This is amazing! I'm not looking for any glory; I make it known to everyone I meet it is because of God. It's just that not many people can claim they went to the Paralympics or Olympics.

I literally have two more weeks of riding. I have to pack my bike on a Friday because I'm leaving on Saturday to a hotel. I decided to stay in Phoenix because I'm leaving early in the morning.

My plane leaves at 5:58 A.M. and I should be there about an hour and a half before I leave. It really wouldn't make any sense to leave my house at 2:45 in the morning and travel down to Phoenix when I could run into a problem and miss my flight.

Time isn't going fast enough for me. I wish I was already there so I could be away from other people who could be sick. I know the pandemic is just as bad there, if not worse than here, but being isolated would be better for me. With this new variant going around, I'm a little worried.

Thinking like this is not helping me. I know God has sent me here; He wouldn't just take it away from me. Although, I prayed that if I allow myself to think I did this by myself to have God take it away from me. I'm not coming close to that because I know God is really the reason why I'm doing this. I tell that to everyone.

Even though I have wonderful days like today, I still wonder if I am going in the right direction. I went for an easy ride today, a recovery ride, so I went to practice turns. As always, I pass out my card and tell people what God has done in my life. I'm not only fulfilling Matthew 28:19: "Therefore go and make disciples of all nations, baptizing them in the name of the Father and of the Son and of the Holy Spirit," but I love doing it. What happened today made me think.

I noticed a man sitting in his car while I was practicing turns in the parking lot. I promised God I would talk to him if he was still there after my last turn. I had this feeling inside me to go talk to him; it was pushing at me. So, I did my final turn and, just as promised, I went to talk with him, and I'm glad I did. I learned he needed prayer because he was going through something.

I just think it's amazing I had this feeling to talk with him. I know as a Christian we are supposed to tell people of the good news and how it is available to everyone. That is why I'm thinking about my direction with cycling. It is amazing to be able to tell people of the good things God has done for me in my life, but I'm supposed to be doing that.

Less than two weeks away until I leave, but not until my first race; I have about three weeks until that. I feel ready. I have beaten all my competitors in the past, so I'm not too worried. I don't want to get overly confident, though. I still must be cautious. I'm still worried but feel incredibly blessed.

My time of departure is drawing near, and with every day my excitement grows stronger. It's still difficult for me to believe I am even going. I believe there are a few different reasons. It's not that I'm good or deserve to go, not at all. I feel it is because I am humble, very thankful, and listened to God when I believe He is talking to me; not audibly, though.

I am, and always have been, very humble about my cycling. I have always felt and told people it wasn't me doing it, and this was before going to the Paralympics. In every race I've ever been in or even when it was just a ride, I made sure people knew it was not me doing it. Even with nonbelievers or others who claim to be and are lying to themselves, I made sure they knew it was God working in me. I have never taken any credit for where I am at, it was me working in agreement with God.

The fact I have been thankful played a huge part in my success, not only for where I am, but also because I'm alive. I would not even be here or doing the things I'm doing without Him keeping me here on earth. I feel my calling in life is to remind people of His love for us through my rehabilitation and giving me my ability.

This whole year has been successful because I have listened to Him. I did not know if I wanted to go to Alabama because of

COVID and all the mandates. I was sure I didn't want to go to Belgium; I had been there many times already. But I'm glad I went to Alabama because it opened a way to go to Belgium, even though I did not want to go. A friend of mine informed me if we went and got on the podium it would add points, aiding us to go to the Paralympics. When I found this out, I wanted to go. When I went to Alabama, I ended coming in second and thought my chances to go were over. But I had prayed to God I would go if He wanted me to, and that's what happened.

My next race was directly after Portugal with no actual rest in between. I got right on the plane and went from Portugal to Minneapolis for the Paralympics time trial. I should have but didn't ride easy while training there. I would have done much better if I'd taken it easier.

The promise I made to God was the main reason I went to Portugal and at the time was not sure I would go to Tokyo. I was sure if I even wanted to go to Tokyo because there was not going to be any spectators watching us. That was until a friend talked me into it. But I still promised God I would go if I was invited. Even though going wouldn't help me be chosen for the Paralympics, I think it did because I came in second.

Today, July 24th, is the first of the trips I've been looking forward to. Although, this year has had a couple trips I've anticipated, with going to Portugal and the other Minneapolis, but the main one had not come yet. I cannot say enough times how much of a complete blessing this year has been.

The only bad thing that happened today, so far, is my flight was delayed. This will mean, more than likely, I will get to my destination later than I thought. I must put my bike together and get ready to go for a ride later which is called a "shake-down" ride. It's to make sure my bike was put together correctly, which may or may not happen.

Just as I didn't know if I would receive in other bad news, or could be good news, my flight from San Francisco to Santa Barbara had been delayed as well. Like I said, I'm not quite sure that is bad news. I won't have to rush to my next plane. It was scheduled to leave at one o'clock, now at 3:20! That is a little long to wait, but it sure is better than missing your flight. Now I'm quite sure I won't be riding today.

I didn't get to the hotel until six, but after I ate dinner, I decided to put my bike together. When Sunday came, I was so happy I decided to stay up and finish building my bike. That night I was getting so frustrated I could not get my chain connected I was about to give up and finish Sunday morning before the ride.

Before we went out on our rides, I was able to talk with a longtime friend of mine I previously mentioned. His name is Ryan Pinney; I met him a while back the Valley of the Sun in Arizona. I told him, "I can't believe we're here. I never dreamed our racing would take us this far. Did you?" I also asked that same question the day before to another friend I had known longer, Freddie De Los Santos. I met him in Redlands before either of us even had the idea we would make this far.

But when Sunday came, I was so glad I could use all my energy for riding. We were traveling to our next hotel in the Santa Ynez Valley from Lompoc. It was only approximately twenty-five miles away, but the way involved climbing, so it was enjoyable. Not that it wouldn't be. This is so much of a blessing for me.

As I sit outside after dinner, I looked back on the team, at all the athletes—the tremendous athletes—and still cannot believe I am one of them. I am an athlete, but I myself don't consider myself on the same level. There are guys on the team who compete and have lost a leg. I am handicapped, but in my opinion, I don't feel as handicapped as they are.

I was supposed to do an endurance ride, which I did, but I also was doing some interval training too. The problem was I had interval training tomorrow and two days of intensive training was going to be extremely difficult. I'm just hoping I'll have enough energy to do it again, and do even better than today. I was unhappy with my performance. It was probably because it took an hour to get where I could do intervals, and I also went very hard up a hill just before I did them.

I was sitting on the patio in my hotel room and thinking about how blessed I am to be here. I was listening in a meeting and all the protocols we have to go through just to go to Japan. Even though there are many rules we have to follow, it is worthwhile. It's amazing I have been chosen to go there; a complete honor.

There aren't many people who get the honor of representing their country, and even better, representing God! I also feel very fortunate to be staying here in the hotel; it's such a nice hotel, over $200 on average a night. I'm sure it's more for us because we get three meals a day and they're not cheap. The first night we were here we had BBQ chicken, and for lunch BBQ steak.

At this hotel I have really met some good people—not athletes, but guests—who are very inspired by us. It gives me a chance to tell my testimony to people.

Like this one man I met on Tuesday, he talked about one of the athletes, Oksana, and how she had never given up and how inspiring she was. To see athletes who overcame their struggles was very inspiring for him, and so many others.

Not just him; there have been many people who wished us well and looked forward to seeing us. I met some young ladies and was able to share what God has done for me. I prefer younger people because they really need to know how good God is. Out of every age I meet, young people are the most important because a lot of them never knew how good God is.

Today had an amazing feeling to it. I went on a thirty-four-mile ride and did not feel tired. Towards the end, yes, I could not wait for it to be over, but I could have gone farther. About mile twenty-five I was going as fast as when I first started, and that was a very good thing. It meant I could go for a longer time at a faster pace, and during the race I would be able to keep a good speed.

It is July 31st, my last day at camp. I still have enough energy to get my final ride in with some intervals. I rode a little too fast in the beginning, but I was still full of energy. To me, this means I will have enough energy to race very well on my second day of racing, even though I will have a day in between.

I am just over three weeks out from traveling over to Japan. I have approximately thirty hours until I go to my final hotel. I will stay one night at the Tokyo Bay Hotel before the Fuji View Hotel. It is approximately a thirteen-hour flight but there are many wait times in between flights. My first layover in San Francisco is five hours.

My two days of travel start early. My first flight leaves from Phoenix at 5:58 A.M. for a quick two-hour flight, but as mentioned, my layover is a lot longer than my flight. Hopefully, I can sneak in a nap between flights because I have a twelve-and-a-half-hour flight to Japan, which I am hoping to get some sleep on. I'm not counting on it because I'm usually unable to sleep on a plane. Although, flying to Portugal, I slept the whole flight because I had a whole row to myself and was able to lie down.

CHAPTER FIFTEEN
A DREAM COME TRUE

Today is the big day, I leave for Tokyo. I have all my paperwork ready and have been training for this moment for the past eight plus years, starting with the recumbent bike. This is something I have always wanted to do and now it can go on my completed list. It's too bad it's in the year of COVID, so my family cannot be there. My support will be overseas, but it will be there, and that is the important thing.

I have to get up very early today, at two, so I am tired, but the excitement of today keeps me awake. I wanted to sleep on the plane, so it really is no problem for me; I wanted to be tired.

I had no problems getting to the airport on time, there was very little traffic, although it did get a little heavier at the airport. But I left in plenty of time; it helped staying close to the airport. I knew it would.

It ended up being a good move because I ran into a little bit of a problem at the check-in desk. It turned out the bike box I normally fly with which holds my bike, was four pounds over, so I had to lighten it. This normally would not be a problem, but it was now around five in the morning and my plane boarded at

5:28 to take off at 5:58. That wouldn't have been much of a problem either, but I also ran into a problem going through security. I had to throw my toothpaste away because you are only allowed a certain amount or ounce size. I ended up rushing there and making pre-boarding just in time, and got right on the plane.

My first flight was less than two hours to San Francisco. The layover was over five hours. It gave me plenty of time to eat and relax before going on my next flight to Tokyo, about ten hours. It did not seem that long because I was able to get some much-needed sleep, about five hours.

When I got to Tokyo, I wasn't ready for what was about to happen next. We were informed we would be going through a quarantine and immigration, but not have to wait over five hours. I was told by a friend I shouldn't complain because I'm going to the Paralympics. That made sense, but I was tired and hungry, so I think it was warranted. The good thing about it was our food was ready when we got to the hotel. Of course, it was very late, about nine thirty, but I was hungry. Besides, I needed to relax and unwind. Since I didn't drink, eating was how I relaxed.

The next day included a two-hour drive to our final hotel, the Fuji View Hotel. The drive didn't seem bad because it was picturesque, so the time ended up going smoothly. I thought I was going to put my bike together, I was talked out of it because I would have had to take it apart and put it back together the next day. It made no sense, so I decided to leave it in the box and ride the trainer. After hearing from my roommate about the ride they went on, it made me wish I would have put my bike together. But that feeling changed when the other athletes had to pack their bikes again.

So, I ended up having a good ride on the trainer today, an hour and a half ride. I approximately rode about eighteen to twenty miles per hour today, which was pretty good considering I didn't want to use all my energy and not get so tired before my race. I knew what speed I was capable of, and it was way too late to try and build my speed up now.

Today, August 26th, was my first day on the track. It's on a raceway for motorcycles. You would think it would be easier to ride. That wasn't the case because it is a technical course: a lot of turns and a couple narrow ones as well. Taking the turns on the racetrack weren't very bad because they were "banked;" the angle of the turn went with the turn. It would be worse if they were in the other direction! But, as stated, it was a very technical course, with some very sharp turns outside of the race course I needed to be careful of.

The problem was the humidity. I wasn't used to riding in that. The heat was something I had to get used to because it really drained my energy. There were two hills, but I only needed to worry about one, although I would do it twice. The other hill was not bad at all, I just needed to be careful not to use all my energy on it the first time. Some of the turns I needed to be very careful of. One of them was horrible because it was right before coming down a huge hill. The hill was only about two tenths of a mile, but the grade was high. It was at least a 50% grade, and I could "catch a pretty high speed. Exactly right after the hill was a sharp right turn under a bridge. If I took it too fast, I'd crash and go right into the wall. I could almost guarantee there would be one crash, especially with the trikes. Right after the second turn, after the bridge, was a sharp ninety-degree turn.

Just on practicing that turn I learned it was very hard. I didn't come close to crashing but it was hard keeping myself from it. I must remember to take the turn slow, so I didn't crash. I wasn't worried about losing any time because I could make it up on ascending the hills. I was very good on them.

The next day was the same, just learning the course for the time trial. It was good to learn the course as much as possible, to know the difficult areas to be aware of. No matter how many times I went over the turn, it didn't seem any easier. I didn't need to practice the road racecourse because it was almost the same course, so being able to practice the time trial course many times was to my advantage.

On August 28th, I was able to try the road racecourse for the first time, and that's all the time I would need since I practiced the other course so much. It was technically not the first time; they were almost the same course. The difference from the time trial course and the road racecourse was there were no sharp turns down the hill and a longer climb. What was worse about it, I needed to do it twice. So today I went four times around the course to acclimate myself to the climb.

I thought yesterday I was riding the full road course, but I was not. The full course included city roads but they couldn't close them off for two days, only for the day of the race. What I missed wasn't much of a big disappointment, it was a couple miles. It was basically a few hills, a few short downhills, a couple straight areas and about ten turns.

What I liked about the course was it had a couple areas where I'd be able to go fast. The downhill would be super-fast, but I still needed to be careful with it and everyone who came near to me. The hill was when I came from the outside streets and back onto the Fuji racetrack area was approximately a two-mile climb; it would be hard the second time. But that was where I exceled over any country. It was like this course was made for me.

But first and foremost, I have to say thank you to God for all of this, it has been a huge blessing. I have come so far along the way, and God has never left my side; He has been there the whole time! Regardless of how this turns out, if I win a medal or not, I am just so thankful to be here. I could not have expected anything that has happened this year. I just made a promise to follow wherever God was going to lead me.

It is the day before my big day, the one I have been waiting for. It is August 30th and about twenty-five plus hours away until the time trial. I am keeping myself relaxed and not trying to over-think or worry too much. I am at peace knowing this has all been determined by God and whatever the outcome, I am joyful. God does not care if I win a medal or what place I come in, that is not why I am here. I'm just sitting in my room now contemplating every turn and every hill, knowing where I need to speed up and where to be careful. I'm also thinking about this opportunity and how blessed I am.

I cannot say that because I lived my life the right way is the reason God answered my prayers, because even before my accident I was not living right. Only about three to four years ago did I start living a better life. Even now, I still have problems. It isn't about living right; it is about faith, and faith is believing God loves you and has a plan for your life!

I believe I was given this gift because God knew exactly what I would do with it. I wasn't going to waste it. He knew I would use it to glorify Him and not myself.

That is why when people say, "Yes, God was involved in this, but a lot of it is you," I quickly correct them and say, "Firstly, if God would not have kept me alive, I wouldn't even be here!" So, He is the only reason I'm here. There are more variables to it, but it was having the faith that God and I agreed, is the main reason I am here.

August 31ˢᵗ, the big day, it is here and time for me to shine!

"You are the light of the world—like a city on a hilltop that cannot be hidden."

Matthew 5:14.

I have been waiting for this opportunity, not to show others I am good, but to show people what God has done for me. It has never been about any glory for me, it has always been about doing this for God. I know where I'm at, there are a lot of people who don't understand my English, but I think they know I ride for God. It will also be televised, so people all over the world can see and know of God's strength and love.

I haven't been nervous at all, not even a little, but now I'm starting to feel a little nervous. I really shouldn't though, because I have "beaten" all these guys before and there are only nine of them.

Last time in Portugal, I was only beaten by one guy here, but the hills are far greater on this course, and I excel on hills. I beat him in Italy, and the hill here is like the one in Italy. All the other guys I beat in both, so I shouldn't be worried, but I also don't want to be overconfident. I need to remain humble. If I get beat, I get beat; just be happy I got to experience this and bring glory to God.

Well, the time is here. I got in my designated start time and ready to race and bring home the gold, but more importantly bring glory to God. I was so "pumped" and the excitement of where I was just made me think of how I got here. The many years of riding a recumbent bike, then training on an upright trike and listening to God prepared me for this. I was one of the last ones to go, so I had about six minutes to think before I took off.

When my time came to leave, I was ushered into the start house, and I had about forty-five seconds before I had to physically ride. But when I finally got to leave, I rode like a banshee. I had approximately the length of one and a half football fields until I had to make my first turn, thankfully most of them were banked. That was the main reason I liked that it was on a racetrack.

I went around a few turns before exiting the track, before the first difficult turn. After that turn, I went about two-hundred feet before I came to that hill and turn I talked about. Even though my bike wanted to go fast, I needed to keep it slow because that sharp turn under the bridge was next; thankfully, I took it with no problems. That was a good thing because about twenty-five feet was the ninety-degree turn I talked about.

After completing that hill and turn, I came to another downhill with another ninety-degree turn. I had trouble with this turn earlier because I was more worried about the other ones. It was no different than the other turn because they both delt with a hill, so I didn't know why I was more worried with the previous turn. This course was very technical, every turn worried me because most were ninety-degree and difficult.

When I think about it, almost all the course was off the track. The course would not have been technical if it remained on the racecourse. Most of the turns were seventy-five to ninety degrees.

I would say ninety percent were off the course because the turns on the track weren't bad at all. It seemed when we started out, we were on the racetrack for about a mile and a half, then it was off the course until toward the end of the course. But there was a very narrow chicane, left and right turn, after the hill on time trial course.

That was where I had my unfortunate accident, on my second lap before the finish. We started about five to ten minutes between the female trike riders, which was why I had my accident. One of the women, who was not in my category, was in my line the way I would normally take. Rather than wait until after the turn, I tried to go around her during. I learned a very important lesson the hard way and ended up crashing. The good thing about it, if there was a good thing, was I did not hurt myself or my bike. I was able to get back up and finish, but I couldn't get my feet back in to my peddles. As a result, I lost a lot of time and watched many people pass me. I ended up coming in ninth, which was last place.

I had the next two days off: one day to ride the bike and one day to completely relax. The day I normally took off, Sunday, I ended up riding because it was the only day to ride the road course before the actual race. I needed to acclimate myself to every turn and the places to be careful about. The hill in the course was huge, approximately two miles long. So, in a way, I was glad I rode the course, but now I wished I hadn't. I take my Sundays off for a Sabbath day of rest, and that was usually a perfect day to rest my muscles.

So, rather than take my normal Sunday off, I ended up taking Monday off so I could be rested for Tuesday's race, it was a big mistake. I normally would keep Sunday holy and important, but I ended putting myself before God. I just spent Monday relaxing at the hotel. I even took a nap outside on the premises. It wasn't raining or humid, so I used the time to pray as well.

It's now September 2nd. Today is the road race and I am a bit nervous. I know I should not be but it's hard not be. I do feel some pressure to perform well but that is really from me, nobody is forcing me. One of the reasons I was invited here is because I'm a great climber, well I used to be. I don't feel like I am anymore. So, I mainly feel pressured by myself. Plus, there is one guy here who has won a medal on the road. It's mainly been women. I feel like I should be the one who should win one as well. This is my last chance to win one, but it is up to God. There is a verse resounding in my head:

> "But as for you, be strong and courageous, for your work will be rewarded."
>
> 2 Chronicles 15:7

I was ready to vindicate myself from the two days before, even though it is raining. The course was different, except we started in the same place, and the distance on the course would be longer. It wasn't as technical as the first one, which made more sense since we would be next to each other. So, I already determined what I would do and how I would achieve success.

To my surprise, I wasn't called last because of my poor performance in the last race. Because of my third-place finish in Belgium, I was the third name called and used the space to the right, next to Spain and Belgium. When we started there still was the football field and a half distance to the first turn. But since it was in the course it was banked. After the turn we went downhill and then another turn. This time there was no chicane.

This time we were on the course about forty percent, but when we were on the roads outside of the course, the turns weren't as bad, except one. Also, I had to do the one turn before the bridge again and in the rain which didn't make it any easier. But when we were in the town, the roads were smooth and fast. There were many turns in the town, but I was only worried about one of them. It was warranted because the rain made it even more difficult, and of course, the turn before the bridge and after. In my past races in Canada, I remembered when I hit the back end of another rider and crashed. I didn't want that to happen again.

Although there was that turn I was worried about, there were a few downhills where I could catch my breath and recover before having to climb up them. When a rider goes down one, they normally climb up one as well. Then, with a few hills and turns, I came to hill I was dreading, the first time with the long hill.

At first, it didn't seem bad, but I was mistaken. I realized I wasn't the hill climber I used to be. I didn't know if it was my age or I was out of shape—more than likely the latter. I was only into the hill probably half a mile and was already winded. One of the parts that really made me feel weak and old was when people I'd beaten before passed me. I had promised myself I wouldn't let that happen.

I passed Spain on the easier part because he passed me on the hard part, but that only happened on the first lap. I realized it was not because he was better, it was because he was saving energy to go up the harder hill. But when I got to the top of that hill, I had to go through the chicane again, the same one I'd crashed on before I was on the straight area that was the pit area for the motorcycle racers.

I learned I wasn't far behind the leaders in the race; they had crashed coming around the first turn before the dangerous hill and turn. So, it was a good thing the guy from Spain passed me—he was in the crash—if I was with them, I would've been in the crash as well. The guy from Spain was having a hard time getting his chain back on. That was a huge advantage for me, but it only lasted for about five to ten minutes, then he passed me again. But I did get to go through the dangerous turns by myself.

He ended up catching me on the downhill, it was probably because we could go very fast, and he was a little more daring than me. On the downhill, we were outside of the track but still on the racetrack grounds, but after the hill was the entrance to the town. This was when I tried to catch up to him, but I couldn't; I could see him, though. I ended staying with the guy from Columbia, Jaunito Betancourt.

He wanted to work with me to try and catch the other racers. I agreed and stayed with him and helped him, until we came to the hill. I really tried to stay with him, but I was losing my energy. I blamed myself, because knowing I was going to the Paralympics, I really should have trained harder. He was half my age and could recover faster than me, but that was just an excuse.

When we got to the top of the hill, I couldn't see him anymore. I saw Spain and tried my hardest to catch him. I was going for fourth place rather than fifth, and almost got it. But I was too out of shape to catch up with him. I was only behind him by about one hundred feet. Regardless of my attempt, I came in fifth place, but it wasn't too bad for a forty-nine-year-old. There is not many people who could say they went to the Paralympics. And if they did, how many could say God sent them there?

Practicing at Fuji Racetrack in late September
Picture taken by Tom Davis

Picture of me during the Road Race at the Fuji Raceway, it was a very dangerous turn. In fact, this picture was taken before the crash of the other riders that I had just missed. August 2021
Picture by Casey Gibson

Fuji Raceway, Japan August 2021
Just before I crossed the finish line, after my crash.
Picture by Unknown

CHAPTER SIXTEEN
WHY I RIDE

We all have doubts sometimes, mine have been very strong lately. I feel I am supposed to be doing this but I am not certain, I know for sure though that God will let me know. I only ride because I have this feeling He wants me to. I know that a door has been open for me. I also feel like having to take the vaccine may be a way to tell me the door is being closed, and another one is being opened. With my prayer being answered a few years back, I really shouldn't doubt.

I have prayed for an answer on this, and I'm not sure if my wondering and worrying about this is my answer. According to one of my Daily Devotionals, we might not hear because we don't like the answer. Now I love to cycle and I desire to bring glory to God through it. I have encouraged many people with my cycling, my story shares with others how good God is. I really do not know why I am doubting and worrying about this.

I feel this is what God wants me to do, but it could be the enemy trying to trick me. I want to bring God glory I think the devil is trying to stop me by tricking me and making me think I am doing this for myself. So in essence, I'm doing this for

God, and I really should continue to do this, but I'm also wondering if this is for myself. I shouldn't feel like I am doing this for myself if I feel God has called me to do this.

I got a feeling inside me today and it was not to give up, do not declare defeat! There are times we can doubt our goals, but it's important if you are doing it right, for God, you will have obstacles in front of you. It's during these times you should feel secure in what you are doing. The devil will try and make you doubt yourself. Whenever you are doing something for God's glory, the enemy tries to throw you off course because he hates that.

I mentioned a man earlier who has suffered from a traumatic brain injury, just as I did. The fact that he is a Christian and wants to ride a bike across America gives me confirmation God sent me to Prescott Valley. As I have said before, God puts people in your life for a certain reason. It is a little too early to know for sure, but it seems like it might be an answer from God.

This is one of the main reasons I want to start a cycling camp; not only to inspire others, but to help them attain their goals. I know if I start my own cycling camp, God will be with me. If this really is confirmation, there's no way I can fail. I know His plans for me will never fail. That's why I'm doing so well with cycling; I believe this was God's plan for me. It took years, I even tried to rush it, which did not work, but when I followed God that was when I did well. Now, with this, I will listen if I'm supposed to do this.

The only explanation I can give is it was God and lots of prayers from many people and myself to Him. Plus, like I already stated, God put this desire and attitude in me to never give up; that is what got me moving from the beginning.

Back when I was home doing nothing, I had the desire to ride a bike again. I just didn't know how I would do it. Feeling that way is how I got started. I didn't know I would do it, but I just told myself I would. That's the way you must be. We are all born with that feeling, but we must use it. God loves us. He does not want us to live a "feeling sorry for myself" kind of life. I knew I was meant for more than just sitting in my wheelchair watching television or being on the computer.

As I said earlier, I wanted to be, and felt I was, an inspiration for people. I thought about becoming a physical therapist, but that wouldn't work because it would require so much school, and I'm not good with school. I knew I wanted to be a light for people to lead them to the true light.

It's up to you and God to make your dreams come true. He puts this desire in you, and sustains that "fire" in you to achieve it. When He gives you a door to walk through, it's up to you to go through it until it's closed or complete. I have been walking through my door for seven years and it isn't finished yet.

I do this out of love for people, to show them how much God loves us by what he has done for me. To show them, despite the person I was, I was still loved and could be used. Despite what people have done in their lives, God can still use them. To show them how loving and caring God is, and to never count Him out! The only thing that matters to me is making sure I bring glory to God; everything I do must do this.

Every day I wake up is a blessing; every day I ride my bike it is a blessing. I can do nothing but honor Him and thank Him. I wouldn't be doing anything without Him. That's why I feel it's not only a desire to do this but as a Christian it's also my obligation.

Something you need to learn is to listen and follow God; He will direct your path. I did not listen, nor did I know how to when growing up and I still have trouble now. You need to go with your feelings because God put those feelings in you, but you need to make sure they are from God.

For example, I had always wanted to be an Olympian, but I became a Para-Olympian. I did not listen well while growing up. Now, I want to be an author, and start a faith-based business in the end. I feel this is what God wants me to do, but I need to make sure these feelings are from God and not myself.

I also worry about taking the vaccine. I worry if it is trusting Man over God; is it God putting men in this world to make a vaccine? But as you can imagine, it is a decision I need to make, but I have a Mighty Counselor I rely on for my answer. This will be a big decision for me to make. I know there are people who look to me to have an answer, but knowing God will give me an answer gives me peace.

God may want me somewhere else and doing something else; I may have had my time cycling for Team USA. This was one door he opened for me, and I can say I obeyed and walked through it. I always said if He didn't want me doing this, to please close the door. Now, if I'm removed from Team USA for not taking the vaccine, I cannot blame Him; I asked for it. This has to do with my faith, believing if I remain on the team, I will continue what I am doing, but if not, another door will be open for me.

Yes, I would like to remain on the team, but only to bring God glory. I don't want to continue racing because I'm excited for the next door God has me walking through, but it could be the same door. There also is a possibility this could also be a waiting period for me to finish this book and afterwards continue racing and bring Him more glory.

The message I heard a few weeks ago about Matthew 25:14-30, the parable about the bags of gold received by the servants and what they did with them, will be true for me because it will describe what I did with all the opportunities He gave me. Either way, if I get the exemption or not, I'm going to bring Him glory.

The Bible states you should work at what you do hard as though you are working for the Lord not other people. So, whether it is racing or doing whatever the Lord has me doing, I'm going to do it for Him. Whatever I do, I will be successful at it because I'm doing it for the Lord, and feel it is what He wants for me.

This is why I decided to go to Tokyo for the Paralympics; I didn't want to go at first. That was also the reason I went to Portugal. I figured if I didn't make to the Paralympics this year, I would at least go to World Championships. I also promised God if I was invited to Portugal, I would go, even if it might hurt my chances going to Tokyo. Very few people understand the promises made to God, and if you do make a promise to Him, you should keep it.

I can submit another appeal to the USOPC because the determination was made by a third party. I can also talk to a lawyer; my church from San Diego is offering to help with this mandate. But I'm questioning the fact I might be trying to keep this door open; am I doing this for me? Or does God have something else He wants me to do? If not, the door He opened for me many years ago will be closed. This might be the case.

Well, tomorrow is the hearing on my appeal. I'm not even worried. I'm wondering if that is a good thing or not. I'm going to miss my friends and flying to different places, but I won't miss the training. I will also miss the money and being able to buy things for my bike and know I'll be repaid; I will probably miss that most.

Today is October 21st and I received some news that could be considered bad. I didn't get my religious exemption, but I can appeal it. That will not be a sure thing, so I'm trying not to worry about it. Besides, God may have another plan for me. Like I've said, what happens in my life is not up out me, the USOPC, or the government; it is up to God.

I'm running into a big quandary here. I don't know if this door is closed and I am still trying to walk through it. I don't like to give up, so I'm not sure if I should try, or just give up. There are two separate avenues to go down but, like I said, I'm not sure if I should quit.

It will be my obligation to believe God will open another door for me, and I know He will. I made a promise to God if I do have to take it, I will retire. The only way I will take it is if God tells me, or that He wants me to take it and keep going. But since He has not told me, I have made the decision I won't take it, even though I won't be on Team USA anymore.

What I plan to do is continue to ride and put my trust in Him. No one, no organization is going to play God with me. Only God has control of any decisions in my life, not the USOPC (the United States Olympic and Paralympic Committee). But, like I said, I'm going to trust whatever the decision made will be His will for me.

God hasn't given me the spirit of fear or the personality of a quitter, but God may have another way for me to go. I'm wondering if seeing a Christian author (Matt) was another door to walk through, or if it was just another extension of the one opened for me years ago.

When I added the sermon, it had me wondering if I should compare myself to the servant who got five bags of gold and keep on going. Cycling and writing would be more than one bag, then if I continue and start my own coaching and then my own cycling camp would be more. I don't want to be the servant with one bag who dug a hole and hid it; if I stayed cycling, that would be me.

If this is God's will for my life, I don't have to worry; I trust Him completely. This may be a test of my faith, to see if I really trust in the Lord. It doesn't mean taking the vaccine to keep cycling to bring Him glory either. I can still cycle and bring Him glory, just not in competition. The trust is doing what I feel is right with Him and will bring Him glory.

I must remember God is in control of all this, Whether I'm on Team USA or go to another Paralympics is not up to me; it is up to Him.

James, Jesus's brother wrote:

> "Now listen, you who say, 'Today or tomorrow we will go to this or that city, spend a year there, carry on business and make money.' Why, you do not even know what will happen tomorrow. What is your life? You are a mist that appears for a little while and then vanishes."
>
> James 4:13

I need to stop worrying about what will happen to me, it is not in my control.

In the past, I have asked God to take it away from me if I wasn't either doing the right thing or becoming too conceited. I will be honest, going to the Paralympics made me feel like a very important person. I tried my hardest to be as modest as I could, but it was difficult. I was thankful to God for letting me get there.

This door may have been closed, and I think it has been. I am not worried about it. I am glad. It may take a little while to get used to it, not having the extra money, but since I don't need to get up and train anymore, that makes me happy. That doesn't mean I will be idle, I just don't have to do it every day and train for a duration. I can go back to having fun again. Not to say I wasn't not having fun, but when you must do something, the fun does dissipate.

I'm not going to give up cycling. I'm not even sure if I'll give up racing. The decision isn't mine to make. It may seem like it right now, but it isn't even the USOPC's decision to make. Only God can make the decisions for me to retire. I may end up wanting to, but if I'm called back to it by God, I will listen.

Today at church, the pastor talked about using your gifts for God's glory and to not worry about how it will affect other people. This is what I have been doing, but I also started to think too highly of myself. This may be time, much needed, to relax and think about different things. Maybe finish working on this book, start a small group, and to work on myself. So, with this on my mind today, I am wondering what it is.

I went back to waiting again, waiting for another door to open. Maybe it has, maybe this one isn't closed. I was wondering if this was a time to rest and take it easy and not to quit cycling all together but not to train as much or as hard as I normally do. So, I'll just be patient and wait and do what I think God wants me to do which is finish writing this book and start a small group.

One of the journeys I went on was to San Diego again. At my old church today, I heard a message I needed to hear. The pastor mentioned how we are never to give up, always be tenacious, even if you fail. Do not give up, God does not want me to quit but be tenacious.

If you are praying about something to happen and aren't

successful, or God tells you "No," that does not mean you weren't supposed to do it, God may be protecting you, or you might be waiting for something, or God may have something better for you.

I don't want to give up, to start giving up. So, whether I get back on Team USA is something I expect or to go another direction, I just have to remember it's not up to me.

So, I'm not at all worried about whether I will be on the team anymore. I don't even think about it. I just ride my bike in the garage, not for anyone, except God, of course. I started for God and for me also, but I did become too high on myself. But now that I've gone as far as I could go, I'm just happy. Do I wish I could keep going? Well, yes, but I'm not going to let it ruin my life. Whether I return will not be up to me, so I choose not to worry about it.

My life isn't over. I need to keep pushing forward and expect greater things to come. Team USA and the Paralympics were an experience I will never forget, but I cannot think of it as only that. Like I said, my life is not over, it is just beginning. I have been "spring-boarded" to the next part of my life, whatever it maybe; I must figure that out. It may be a couple different things: it may be this book or getting back on Team USA. I do not know. One thing I'm sure of is my purpose. It is my passion, and I believe my responsibility, to tell people what God has done for me, and do it with enthusiasm.

I have been doing some thinking about my next decision, and it has to do with cycling, but it's regarding my past experiences. It starts with the completion of this book, but it would only be a beginning. It has to do with my website, but turning it into a business. I have wanted to make my site into a business but have always wondered how I would do it. Just as I mentioned the parable about the bags of gold, I also want the cycling camp as well.

Even though I assume it is over, I still find myself wondering why this happened to me. I can walk away from this whole journey, and the reason is because I feel my job is complete. I was doing this to bring people closer to God, and I feel I have. I know it is more than one person, but whatever the number, I did do it.

I have always wanted to hear God say to me when my life is over, "You were a good and faithful servant."

I feel that way. This just makes me feel accomplished. It isn't about how much money I make, how many houses I have, or what car I drive. I just do this so people can find the joy I have, to understand where I got this joy.

CHAPTER SEVENTEEN
A FINAL WORD

Whether or not I'm done with racing or going to the next Paralympics is of no concern to me; it isn't even my decision. Would I go if I got the chance to go to the Paralympics? Well, yes, that is only because I believe God would want me to go. I keep training because He may make that decision for me to continue.

If I were honest with you, I don't want to race or go to the Paralympics; it does take a lot of work. If God wants me to go, I will obey, that has already been decided. I have spent around eight plus years of my life to get to the Paralympics. I never thought I would go, but I did. That's why I can walk away from it.

I don't know what the future holds, I just keep my tenacity, knowing God already has something planned for me. It is already predetermined, just like this whole journey I was on, although everything that happens could be the same journey. That is why it is very important to have faith, knowing God already has everything worked out for you.

So, if I race again, I race, but all that matters to me is making sure God gets the glory. That is all I ever wanted, but with going to the Paralympics I lost that. I have learned the outcome of going to Tokyo did not matter to God; the fact I went and He sent me is what mattered. In the very beginning, yes, I wanted to be on Team USA, I wanted to go to the Paralympics, I wanted to do this for myself, but that has all changed.

I have had many people who have either offered me condolences or were upset I was removed from Team USA because I would not take the vaccine. What I always tell people is that, "I am not upset; I am because of the health workers and the governmental employees like police officers and such who have families, but not for me. I got to go to places most people will never visit. I got to go to the Paralympics. I was able to do what I was made to do, that is bring glory to God with my cycling." Not many people can say they lived a good life. I can.